KEN PYE

MORE MERSEYSIDE TALES

KEN PYE

MORE MERSEYSIDE TALES

CURIOUS & AMAZING TRUE STORIES

FROM HISTORY

First published 2016

The History Press
The Mill, Brimscombe Port
Stroud, Gloucestershire, GL5 2QG
www.thehistorypress.co.uk

British Library Cataloguing in Publication Data.
A catalogue record for this book is available from the British Library.

ISBN 978 0 7509 7052 5

Typesetting and origination by The History Press
Printed and bound in Great Britain by TJ International Ltd

CONTENTS

ACKNOWLEDGEMENTS

I certainly hope that you enjoy this new collection of Merseyside tales, and there are still so many more where these came from!

Of course, it would not be possible to produce such a broad collection of stories without help and support. I would therefore like to thank the staff of Liverpool Central Libraries and the Liverpool Record Office in particular; and the librarians and many of my fellow proprietors of the Liverpool Athenaeum.

I would also like to acknowledge the support and stories given to me by the Earl of Derby DL; the late Sir Alan Waterworth KCVO; Mumin Khan of the Abdullah Quilliam Heritage Centre; the Most Reverend Justin Welby, Archbishop of Canterbury and former Dean of Liverpool Anglican Cathedral; Ken Rogers, journalist and author; John Illingsworth, former governor of HM Prison Liverpool; Richard MacDonald, of the Reader Organisation; the late Professor Richard Codman III and Julia Lisman. I am, as always, very grateful for their encouragement, time and friendship.

Introduction

In my first volume, *Merseyside Tales*, I stated just how proud I am of being a born and bred Scouser, but one who has worked all over Merseyside, now renamed as Liverpool City Region, and who loves the entire county with an abiding passion. One of the many things that make this part of the world so attractive for me, apart from its wonderful people, is its rich and diverse heritage. Whilst I find this endlessly fascinating I am particularly entertained and continuously amazed by the wealth of tales from its history that are odd, unusual, surprising or simply bizarre.

This is the second volume in my series of such stories, and I know that I have found another fifty of them that I am sure will entertain, delight, and hopefully surprise you too. As with volume one, all of my stories are true (although some are more true than others), and they all prove that truth is stranger than fiction.

I certainly hope that you enjoy reading them, just as much as I enjoyed researching and writing *More Merseyside Tales*.

Ken Pye
Liverpool, 2016

THE NAUGHTY NYMPHETTE OF NESTON

In 1765 on 26 April, Emily Lyon was born in Neston to the local blacksmith and his wife, and the family home still survives in the former fishing village. Emily's father died not long after his daughter's birth, leaving his widow and baby impoverished. So Mrs Lyon took her child to her hometown of Hawarden in North Wales, where she grew into a spirited, independent and astoundingly good-looking teenager with a very casual attitude towards sex and relationships. This meant that she was a challenge to bring up, but Emily was destined to have an interesting and unusual life.

When her daughter reached the age of 15 Emily's mother decided that she should go to London to seek her fortune. Here, she first took a position as a nursery maid, but soon met a failed medical student from Edinburgh by the name of James Graham (1745–94). He was impressed by her beauty and immediately offered Emily employment in his brand new 'Temple of Health', which he had opened in fashionable Pall Mall, in August 1779.

Here, and for a fee of 2 guineas, his patrons wandered through ornately furnished rooms festooned with glittering arrays of artificial flowers, and could also breathe in the heady, beeswax perfumed air. Throughout this curious establishment the sounds of delicate music could be heard, played on violins, harps, harpsichords, cymbals and tambourines. They could also listen to Graham delivering lectures on health and buy his patent medicines.

Patrons of the Temple of Health were also exposed to very scantily clad young men and women, including Emily (now known as 'Emma'), who were called 'Gods and Goddesses of Health' and wafted rhythmically in time to the music in and around the candlelit rooms and passageways. These creatures draped themselves provocatively against exotically coloured life-sized, nude, male and female Grecian and Romanesque statues. These young dancers were described by Graham as being 'examples of physical perfection' whose purpose was to encourage his clients to get into a more erotic mood!

By the end of 1780, the Temple of Health was so successful that Graham was turning away carriages from his door on a regular basis, and demand for his full range of services was in full swing. Customers were encouraged to experiment with strange contraptions and appliances described by Graham as 'medico-electrical apparatus'.

Amongst Graham's collection of pseudo medical equipment was the main attraction, his 'Electric Celestial Bed'.

Electricity had just been discovered and its use as a medical aid had become all the rage, especially amongst the 'idle rich' and those members of the rising middle classes who were particularly concerned about establishing a personal bloodline!

For a fee of £50 a night, couples seeking to produce children would undress and lie on the bed, then have various parts of their bodies wired up. They would be subjected to a series of 'stimulating electrical impulses and energising vibrations' that were said to be designed to 'encourage the libido and strengthen their amorous capacity'. Graham advertised that anyone who spent even one night in his 'medico, magnetic, musico, electrical bed' would be 'blessed with progeny', and 'sterility or impotence would be cured completely'.

A newspaper report of the day described the bed as:

A wonder-working edifice, 12 feet by 9 feet. Its mattress is filled with sweet, new-mown wheat and oat straw; mingled with balm, rose leaves, and lavender flowers; as well as with hair from the tails of fine English stallions.

Overhead is a domed canopy, covered in fresh flowers and animated, musical, mechanical figures.

Stimulating oriental fragrances and ethereal gases are released from a reservoir inside the dome, from which is suspended, above the passionate couples, a large mirror that allows lovers to observe themselves entwined in amorous abandon.

A tilting inner frame puts couples in the best position to conceive, and their movements set off music from organ pipes, which breathe out celestial sounds, whose intensity increases with the ardour of the bed's occupants.

So, the more you moved, the more the bed moved, and the more musical and perfumed it became. I don't know about you, but I would find all this a bit of a distraction really!

In the Temple of Health, Emma Lyon soon became renowned as the most special of Graham's beautiful bevvy of nubile young women, and was now titled the temple's 'Vestal Virgin'. Soon after taking up her position (if that is the most appropriate term!) at Graham's bizarre emporium, Emma became renowned about London and the Home Counties for her beauty, and she had no difficulty attracting suitors. These often titled gentlemen soon introduced her to a much more sophisticated lifestyle. In fact, before long she became the mistress of Sir Harry Featherstonehaugh (1754–1846) of Uppark. However, in 1781, and at the age of only 16, she became pregnant but Sir Harry refused to support her or the child; perhaps he doubted that the baby was actually his.

Fortunately for Emma, though, she was quickly taken as the mistress of Sir Charles Greville (1749–1809), the second son of the Earl of Warwick, but he insisted that her baby be sent back to the Wirral where it was then looked after by Emma's family. Sir Charles now improved his young lover's social skills, developed her education, and taught her how to sing, dance and act with some genuine talent. Emma now became the toast of London society and of the aristocracy, and she began to be invited to salons, levées, afternoon teas, weekend house parties, balls and the opera.

In 1784, and now aged 19, Emma was introduced to Charles Greville's uncle, Sir William Hamilton (1730–1803), who was the British ambassador to the Court of Naples. But, two years later and badly in debt, Greville reached an agreement with his wealthy and influential relative: in exchange for Hamilton settling all of Greville's debts, Emma was sent to Naples to become his uncle's mistress. This relationship was a surprising success and Emma began to make friends with the Neapolitan royal family. She also had quite some influence at court. In 1791, Emma and Sir William married, and the erstwhile exotic dancer from Neston became Lady Emma Hamilton. She was only 26 years old, whilst her husband was 60.

Then, in 1798, Rear Admiral Sir Horatio Nelson (b. 1758) was visiting the King and Queen of Naples when Emma caught the

Emma on her wedding day to Sir William Hamilton, 6 September 1791.
Emma was then 26 years old. (Liverpool Athenaeum library)

sailor's eye (this was quite fortunate really as he only had one!). The
popular and renowned naval officer and the still stunningly beautiful
Emma were immediately drawn to each other. They fell deeply and
passionately in love and began an affair. This very quickly became
public knowledge as they were anything but discreet. However, the
great naval hero was already married, and although this relationship

had broken down Nelson's relationship with Lady Emma Hamilton, who was of course still very publicly married to Sir William, now grew into a great scandal. Even so, Sir William was amazingly compliant, knowing full well about his wife and Nelson.

In 1801, Emma Hamilton bore Nelson a daughter, whom they named Horatia. Even though their relationship outraged the public, because of Nelson's outstanding reputation and status in the country, British society pretended to find Emma and her affair with Nelson perfectly acceptable. But behind her back she was reviled and the subject of persistent and malicious gossip. Emma remained oblivious to this until Nelson was killed at the Battle of Trafalgar, on 21 October 1805. When the news was brought to her, Emma screamed and fell into a dead faint, and could not speak for almost a day. She later wrote, 'Life to me is not worth having. I lived for him. His glory I gloried in … But I cannot go on. My heart and head are gone.'

In his will, Lord Nelson left Emma a small legacy of £800, and also as a 'bequest to the nation' asking that his friends, and British society, should continue to welcome and support her. However, society very quickly cast Emma aside and excluded her from the lifestyle that she had become so used to. The bereaved Emma soon found that she had many debts and the legacy was soon spent. In fact, by the spring of 1808, she owed more than £8,000.

In 1813, she was arrested for debt and spent time in the King's Bench Prison in Southwark, although because of young Horatia she was allowed to live in some very dismal rooms nearby. Emma was drinking heavily by now and was subject to long bouts of severe depression. In 1814, what friends she did have left had raised enough money to smuggle her and Horatia, now aged 13, to Calais in France. Here, they lived in cramped and poor lodgings where, according to Horatia, her mother spent the days lying on her bed drinking herself into a stupor – but not for long. In 1815 and at the age of only 50, Emma Lyon, the former exotic dancer from Neston and one-time Lady Hamilton, died an alcoholic in dire poverty, probably of cirrhosis of the liver. She was buried in the local church of St Pierre in Calais, which later became the Parc Richelieu. Here, in 1994, a memorial was erected to this tragic woman from the Wirral.

The Goddess Minerva

On the top of the dome of Liverpool's grand and glorious Town Hall, with its four clock faces flanked by lions and unicorns, sits the statue of the goddess Minerva – the Roman equivalent of the Greek goddess, Athena. She sits in powerful and benevolent guardianship over the city and, as the goddess of wisdom, warfare, strength, science, magic, commerce, medicine, teaching, creativity, the arts and poetry, and as the inventor of spinning, weaving, numbers and music, she is a perfect symbol of Liverpool – 'the world in one city', a European Capital of Culture, and an internationally renowned World Heritage port.

The people of Merseyside, and of Liverpool in particular, certainly know how to celebrate life and community, and some of the most famous people in the world have visited our Town Hall over the centuries. They have come here for balls, presentations, official receptions and grand formal dinners. Most of these dignitaries, including royalty, seem to have succumbed to the power of the city to encourage self-expression and self-indulgence.

This is why, on the list of people who have had to be carried, or in some cases dragged, out of the Town Hall more than a little worse for wear, you will find Mark Twain (1835–1910), author of *Tom Sawyer*; King Edward VII (1841–1910); General Ulysses S. Grant (1822–85), US Army general and president; and a young William Ewart Gladstone (1809–1898), who later became prime minister four times.

Prince William Frederick (1776–1834), Duke of Gloucester and Edinburgh, also celebrated rather too well at the Town Hall. This was at a civic function in 1803, after which the prince was quoted in the local press as saying, 'by the time of the 24th toast, the entire hall had lost count of the proceedings'. Even the Duke of Clarence (1765–1837) got 'falling down drunk' at a formal reception in the building on 18 October 1806. Some reports said that he was carried out singing to his carriage on Dale Street. Also known as 'Sailor Bill' and 'Silly Billy', on 26 June 1839 he ascended the throne as King William IV!

However, one visitor to Liverpool Town Hall had very little cause to celebrate. On 6 November 1865, Commander James Waddell (1824–86), the captain of the American Confederate warship, CSS

The goddess Minerva sits on the dome of Liverpool Town Hall in benevolent guardianship of the people of the city. (Discover Liverpool library)

Shenandoah, came into the main entrance of the imposing building. In his hand he carried a letter addressed to Liverpool's Lord Mayor, surrendering his vessel to the British government. Earlier that day he had lowered the Confederate flag aboard his ship and formally handed his vessel over to Captain Poynter of HMS *Donegal*, mid-river on the Mersey. This was the last official act of the American Civil War (1861–65), which therefore ended, not in America, but in Liverpool.

The goddess Minerva gazed down on all these proceedings in silent, perhaps amused benevolence.

LIFESAVING AND CURRANT BUNS

As shipping on the River Mersey increased during the eighteenth century, it became necessary to build navigation aids and hazard warnings to guide vessels as they sailed in and out of the dangerous estuary. By 1763, there were two lighthouses on the Leasowe shore, but one of these was badly damaged in severe weather. This was replaced in 1771 by a new lighthouse re-sited on the top of Bidston Hill – not the present building on the hill, though.

The remaining lighthouse, which is the one still standing at Leasowe today, carries the date stone inscribed 'MWG 1763', which commemorates the then Mayor of Liverpool, William Gregson. Inside there is a well-preserved cast-iron staircase, which is believed to be contemporary with the building.

The lighthouse once also acted as the clubhouse for the Leasowe Golf Club, which was established in 1891, when a course was laid out on the common land around the building. The golf club moved to its

Leasowe Lighthouse. (Discover Liverpool library)

present site, adjacent to Leasowe Castle, in 1893. In 1894, Mr and Mrs Williams, who had been keepers of the lighthouse on the Great Orme at Llandudno, transferred to Leasowe. Sadly, shortly after they moved, Mr Williams died and the Mersey Docks and Harbour Board, who had responsibility for the building, made Mrs Williams one of the first female lighthouse keepers in the country.

When the lamp was finally turned off and the lighthouse ceased to operate, on 15 July 1908, Mrs Williams moved into a cottage nearby. But the enterprising widow kept the lighthouse as a teahouse, serving 'teas, minerals and light refreshments' to summer visitors and, on Sunday afternoons, to golf club members. This service was extremely popular and her currant buns were said to be particularly scrumptious.

In 1929, Leasowe Lighthouse was put up for sale, but was not disposed of until 1930, when Wallasey Corporation bought it for £900. Mrs Williams died in 1935, and the lighthouse was closed to the public, boarded up and no longer used. It became a local curiosity and remained a popular landmark until the setting up of the North Wirral Coastal Park in 1989, when it once again began a new lease of life as the Ranger Station and Information Centre. Leasowe Lighthouse is now open to the public and is well worth a visit.

HENGLER'S CIRCUS AND THE HIPPODROME

On West Derby Road and facing the end of Everton Road, just east of Liverpool city centre, is a builder's yard on an area of semi-derelict land. Those who know nothing of what once stood here simply drive or walk past without giving it a second's thought. And yet, this was the site of two of Liverpool's most famous places of entertainment – Hengler's Grand Circus and 'the Hippy'.

Henry Hengler (1784–1861) was a famous circus performer throughout Britain during the late eighteenth and early nineteenth centuries, and his son, Frederick Charles Hengler (1820–87), known as Charles (and also as 'Handsome Hengler'), followed in his father's footsteps. Charles first became a 'rope dancer', which was another term for tightrope walker, and then gained a popular reputation as a skilled horseman, performing with a number of touring circus troupes. But

Charles had always wanted to branch out on his own so, in 1848, he opened his own spectacular, touring, tented show, known as 'Hengler's Cirque'.

Soon, he realised that it would be far more efficient, and profitable, to have permanent shows in the larger cities around the country. So he began to acquire spacious buildings that could be redesigned and converted to accommodate his particular form of spectacle and entertainment. In 1863, Hengler bought the old Prince's Theatre in West Nile Street in Glasgow, followed by equally grand premises in Edinburgh, Dublin, Hull, London and, of course, Liverpool.

In the great port, with its rapidly increasing population of people craving diversion and distraction from their often hard way of life and work, Charles constructed his first circus building on Dale Street. This was a large, single-storey, circular theatre built entirely of wood and canvas. It stood on the site of the old Saracen's Head Inn, which had once been one of Liverpool's most important coaching inns. This had been demolished in 1855, and Hengler's Grand Cirque gave their first performance in their new building on 16 March 1857.

With acrobats of all types, horse riders, animal trainers and clowns, the people of Liverpool were thrilled and delighted by what they saw at the Cirque. A contemporary description of the theatre reads:

> Hengler's Cirque Varieties has opened, in Dale Street … a handsome, commodious, and spacious theatre, devoted to equestrian performances, which has been constructed by Messrs Holmes and Nicol of this town, on the model of Franconi's famous Cirque, in the Champs Elysees, Paris.
>
> The building, though of a temporary character, is most admirably suited for the purpose for which it is designed; and while accommodating an immense number of spectators, who can all easily witness the performances, the ventilation is perfect, and with an entire absence of draughts. There is nothing to offend the senses of smell or sight.
>
> The audience is placed in compartments round the circle; the frequenters of the boxes being seated on cushioned chairs, with a carpeted flooring under their feet. The compartments entitled 'pit' and 'gallery' are also very comfortable, while round the whole building runs a spacious promenade.

The ceiling is covered with coloured folds of chintz, which give a brilliant and cleanly appearance; and the pillars supporting the roof are neatly papered, and ornamented with flags and shields. The whole aspect is, in fact, what has long been a desideratum in this country, and we regret it will have to be pulled down again in a few months.

And so it was, because in 1861, the ground on which Hengler's building stood was sold and the ambitious impresario had to find a new site for his very successful show. The circus troupe gave their final performance on Dale Street on 14 March 1861, and Liverpool City Council's former municipal buildings now stand on this site.

Undaunted, Charles Hengler soon found a new location in the town, on a street named Newington, which still runs between Renshaw and Bold Streets. With incredible speed, and with equally incredible expenditure, he constructed a brand new specially designed and lavishly decorated circus building. A newspaper report of the time said that the new cirque was of 'greater magnificence and more complete than anything of its kind erected in Great Britain'.

Just seven months after moving from Dale Street, in October 1861 the fabulous New Grand Cirque Varieté opened its doors to an expectant public. They were not disappointed because the show was just as impressive as its advance publicity had promised. This was because Charles Hengler was not just a gifted showman in the sawdust ring but in print, too. He paid for sensational printed advertisements, posters and handbills, which announced 'Great Novelties' and 'Screaming Comic Scenes'. They also promoted exhibitions of 'horsemanship of the highest order' presented by 'Mr Williams' who made 'astounding leaps'.

The public were also invited to see 'Miss Emily Cooke' execute 'exquisite poses of grace and beauty', and to witness special appearances of 'Mr John M. Hengler' (1831–1919), one of Charles' three sons, to perform outstanding feats of physical dexterity on the '*corde elastique*'. This was a tightrope secured at both ends by springs, which gave it 'bounce', enabling the acrobat to execute complicated leaps and somersaults.

Hengler was also a pioneer of Christmas pantomimes, which were proving to be extremely popular in Victorian England. In 1863,

A riotous pantomime in full and watery flow in Hengler's
Circus. (Discover Liverpool library)

he presented daily matinee and evening performances of 'Brilliant
Equestrian and Gymnastic Acts', followed by a show with the
magnificent title of 'Blue Beard, or Harlequin King of Mischief, and
the Fairy of the Coral Grotto'.

This featured dazzling, gloriously decorated and illuminated scenes,
state-of-the-art special effects and fabulous costumes, as well as a large
cast of very dramatic actors and actresses. Its impact on audiences
was unprecedented and they came to see this show in their tens of
thousands. Ticket prices for the boxes and best seats sold for three
shillings each, and sixpence for seats in the gallery; children were
charged at half price.

After only seven years at Newington, Hengler once again had to
close down his grand circus building. This time it was to make way for
the new Central Station and train tracks of the Cheshire Lines Railway.
In 1870, Hengler closed his theatre and, failing to find another site that
suited his ambitious standards, decided to move away from Liverpool
– but not for long. Large, approving audiences and therefore huge
profits were always guaranteed in the great sea port, so in 1876, Charles

Hengler returned to Liverpool. He opened his latest Grand Cirque on West Derby Road, just on the edge of the district of Everton, on 13 November 1876. This lavish new building had been designed by the well-known theatre architect, Jethro T. Robinson (d. 1878). A feature of the show was a water spectacular, in which the circus ring would be flooded with 23,000 gallons of water in just thirty-five seconds!

For another twenty-five years Hengler's Grand Cirque continued to entertain the Liverpool public with stunning and complex productions, as well as with circuses and pantomimes; all with performing animals, acrobats, high-flying trapeze artists and clowns. This was even though Charles Hengler had died in 1887. However, by the end of the century, audience numbers were tailing off as tastes changed.

In 1901, Hengler's Grand Circus building was closed so that it could be completely redesigned, now by the renowned theatre architect, Bertie Crewe (1860–1937). In August 1902, it reopened as the Royal Hippodrome Theatre of Varieties. Gloriously reconstructed in a sumptuous Louis XV style, and increased in size to make the lobby and auditorium more spacious. Not only were there tiered balconies and boxes, but it could seat 3,500 people, with space for another 500 standing. The high, circular ceiling featured painted panels by the artist Walter Sickert (1860–1942). Above the proscenium arch were five more painted panels representing the five senses.

The inaugural programme began with the very large orchestra playing the National Anthem. This was followed by ten variety acts that were headlined by the renowned troupe of acrobats, the Sisters Dainaff. For the next twenty years, the Royal Hippodrome provided the people of Liverpool with thrills as well as with top quality music hall entertainment, which was often spectacular and always popular.

Among the stars to appear here were the great escapologist, Harry Houdini; the miniature clown with giant boots, Little Tich; Charlie Chaplin, before he became the internationally famous star of silent film comedies; Gracie Fields; Fred Karno's comedy dancing troupe; and the popular Liverpool-born comedians, Rob Wilton and George Robey. George Formby Senior also appeared here, as did the handsome and powerful weightlifter, the Great Hackenschmidt. It was during this time that the popularity of the theatre resulted in it becoming known affectionately as 'the Hippy'.

In June 1931, following further changes in public tastes, the theatre closed. The Hippy's last night as a music hall was a sentimental, extravagant and boisterous affair. The programme included the famous and popular music hall stars Harry Champion, singing 'Any Old Iron', and Vesta Victoria, singing 'Waiting at the Church'.

One month later, the Hippy reopened as a cinema with the number of seats now reduced to 2,100, and with a presentation of the early Universal Studios horror film, *Dracula*. This played to over 30,000 people in the first week, and it is said that the star of the film, Bela Lugosi (1882–1956), came to Liverpool to promote his film at this time. However, the author has yet to find any evidence to support the claim.

The Royal Hippodrome Cinema remained a popular venue for Scousers for the next four decades, and in 1959, as an 8-year-old boy, I remember being taken to the Hippy by my mother, to see the double feature of *Tom Thumb* and *The Wizard of Oz*. I was dazzled by the magic of both films, shown as they were in the exotic surroundings of the Hippy, with its blue and white plaster mouldings, swags of drapery, naked cupids in every corner and lush, velvet curtaining. I also remember falling in love a little with Judy Garland!

However, the local population of the area declined during the late 1960s, and the Royal Hippodrome closed on 16 May 1970. Its final film was *Winning*, starring Paul Newman, but the old building did not win and it lay unused and derelict until 1984, when sadly the once famous and much-loved Hippy was demolished.

The Real Inventor of the 'Mighty Wurlitzer'

The world-famous Wurlitzer Theatre Organ was manufactured and produced by the Wurlitzer Company in New York, USA. However, they did not invent this remarkable, self-contained orchestra. It was the creation of Robert Hope-Jones, who had been born on 9 February 1859 at Hooton Grange, Cheshire, which lies between Chester and Birkenhead.

The family was wealthy and musical, and young Robert developed an enthusiastic interest in music as a child. This was encouraged by his parents and he developed this whilst studying at Birkenhead School. He also became an accomplished organist, playing regularly at church as well as at home. However, Robert also had a serious interest in engineering and upon leaving school he began an apprenticeship at Laird's shipbuilders, also in Birkenhead.

Two of the great technological developments of the age were the electric telegraph and the telephone and, in 1881, Robert gave up his job with Laird's to join a brand new organisation, the Lancashire & Cheshire Telephone Company. Here he entered into his new career with passion and dedication, and he was soon promoted to the position of chief engineer with the company. Robert learned much during his time there, especially about the developing science of electronics. He also decided to combine his love for music with his technological skills and, at work and at home, he began experimenting with an electrically driven system for delivering air to pipe organs.

Previously, mechanical bellows had to be manually pumped to create the wind pressure to produce the music from organ pipes, now Robert could do this using electric motors and pneumatic pumps. He was so successful with his experimental designs that between 1890 and 1914 he took out more than forty patents in both Britain and America.

It was at this point that Robert decided to go into business for himself and, in 1892, the Hope-Jones Electric Organ Company of Birkenhead was created to turn his designs into practical instruments. Controversially, he employed women to work in his factory, which caused the men in his workforce to immediately go on strike.

Not only was he bad at industrial relations but he was also no accountant. He seldom paid his bills on time and was always being hounded by creditors and disgruntled investors. Nevertheless, his technical and inventive skills were remarkable, as were the sophisticated electrically driven pipe organs that he was now producing.

Eventually, though, he realised that he had to close down his now failing Birkenhead business completely and, in 1903, he and his wife emigrated to America. Sailing aboard the SS *Teutonic* from Liverpool, he arrived in New York on 7 May 1903. Despite his recent experiences and his business ineptitudes (which he failed to acknowledge or overcome), Robert immediately opened a new business in the town of Elmira in New York, building electro-pneumatic pipe organs. Here, he developed the idea of constructing a complex organ, comprising not only a vast array of pipes but also many other instruments and sound effects. He also invented a system that allowed this device to be installed in theatres, behind great louvred screens which projected the sound around even the largest auditoriums.

Robert Hope-Jones, the real inventor of the 'Mighty Wurlitzer'. (Discover Liverpool library)

Not only this, but his organ could be played remotely from a separate console at the stage, connected to the main instrument by electric cables. Robert also developed the idea of special stop tabs to control the volume of the complex organ, as well as the vast variety and combinations of instruments it could imitate and sounds that it could produce.

Sadly, if predictably, this business began to fail too; but rescue was at hand, or so Robert thought. In 1910, he visited the Wurlitzer Company at their manufacturing headquarters in North Tonawanda, New York, and they were very impressed by his ideas and inventions. They were also charmed by Robert's manner and encouraged by his undoubted technical skill. Enthusiastically, if naively, Robert agreed to enter into partnership with the organ builders, and a new company was formed, named The Wurlitzer Hope-Jones Unit Orchestra.

Too late, Robert eventually realised that he had, in fact, effectively signed over the rights to all his inventions, ideas and patents to the American company. He became extremely depressed by the loss of all ownership and credit for his remarkable invention and found it impossible to continue working with his American partners. In fact, they were paying him $50 a week to stay out of the factory!

Using gas piped to a lamp behind an organ console in a New York church, on 13 September 1914, and at the age of only 55, Robert Hope-Jones, the real inventor of the 'Mighty Wurlitzer', committed suicide.

WILLIAM HUTCHINSON – LIVERPOOL'S REMARKABLE DOCK MASTER

William Hutchinson was an extremely gifted man, as well as being a fascinating character. He was a sailor, privateer captain, ship owner and merchant, shipwright, inventor, scientist, author, local politician, health pioneer and philanthropist. Also, and most significantly, he was appointed as Liverpool's first dock master and its principal water bailiff.

William had been born in 1715 in Newcastle-upon-Tyne and, following the unexpected death of his father in 1727, at the age of only 11 he was forced to seek work at sea. He took a job as cabin boy, cook and beer drawer for the sailors aboard a collier ship. This was a coastal trader carrying much needed coal from the north-east of England to London and the south.

In 1738, at the age of 23, he became, in his own words, 'a 'fo'c'sle man on an East Indiaman, sailing to India and China'. Two years later, in 1740, William decided to permanently move to Liverpool, where he knew that the opportunities for ambitious young seafarers were much better.

By 1743 he was in the Royal Navy, serving as mate on a 'bomb's tender' ship, operating out of Hyeres Bay near Marseille. This was a life-threatening job, because the War of the Austrian Succession

The inventive and pioneering William Hutchinson.
(Liverpool Athenaeum library)

(1740–48) was then being fought and a bomb's tender was a vessel used for carrying stores and ammunition to warships, which were known in the navy as 'bombs'.

With the sea now completely 'running through his veins', and as an experienced and skilful seafarer, in 1746 William served aboard the *Perl*, a West Indiaman that had been fitted out as a privateer. He had been issued 'letters of marque' by the British Government, which gave him authority to take an armed ship to 'attack, capture and plunder' enemy merchant ships in time of war. In other words, he was a legalised, government-sanctioned pirate, and the current targets were the merchant vessels of France and Spain. However, and in an already eventful and exciting life, William and his crew were captured and taken prisoner by a French squadron, but fortunately he was released shortly afterwards.

In 1747, he took command of another privateer, the *St George*, capturing the French ship, *St Jean*. In 1750, he joined forces with Wallasey-born Fortunatus Wright (1712–57), who was already Merseyside's most colourful, famous and successful privateer captain – but his is another story …

The Hutchinson–Wright partnership was astoundingly profitable for both men, and for their crew. Aboard the ex-Royal Navy, twenty-gun frigate *Lowestoft*, Hutchinson captured many foreign merchant ships. These vessels and their often rich cargoes were then either ransomed back to their countries of origin or sold at auction. As a result both men made themselves very wealthy. Indeed, by 1752 Hutchinson was rich enough to build his own boat, especially designed for privateering and trade in the West Indies. Also, in 1755 the Corporation of Liverpool made him a Freeman of the Town.

But it was not all plain sailing for William. In his memoirs William wrote how he and his crew had been shipwrecked in a severe storm and had to take to the lifeboat. They were adrift and far from land, and soon the food supplies ran out. After some debate they had to accept that the only way to survive was to eat one of their number. They agreed to draw lots to choose who would sacrifice himself and, unfortunately, William lost. He then wrote of how he prayed and made his peace with God, and was just about to be slaughtered by his crew when a ship was spotted on the horizon.

To everybody's relief, not least of all William's, the men were picked up and saved. Ever afterwards, William, who was a quietly religious man of Puritan leanings, set aside the date of his rescue as a day of private prayer and thanksgiving. Indeed, his Christianity meant that William would not tolerate any ribald or coarse behaviour aboard his ships, and especially swearing of even the mildest kind. This must have made life difficult for the salty old seadogs and sons of the sea who were his crewmen.

Naturally, this adventure had now made the saltwater in William's veins run a little colder, and he decided to forsake the sea and spend the rest of his life on land in his adopted town. In 1758, Liverpool Corporation were looking for an experienced professional to oversee the management and organisation of its expanding dock network and, in 1759, they offered William Hutchinson the post of dock master. William accepted, and retained this position for twenty years. He also became water bailiff, which was an important post that had its origins in Norman times.

However, after only three months in the job, William had yet another brush with death. For reasons that are not known, whilst on the dockside William was suddenly approached by an enraged sailor. The man's name was Murphy, and he was a seaman aboard the privateer ship, *New Anson*. Murphy came right up to William, yelled out, 'Damn you, you are a villain!', pointed a pistol directly at the dock master and pulled the trigger. It was only due to the fact that the weapon misfired that William avoided a possibly fatal injury, giving bystanders the opportunity to grab Murphy and take him into custody. The disgruntled seaman was later sentenced to serve in the Royal Navy for the rest of his life, which, in the navy of those times, could often be a fate worse than death.

During his time as Liverpool's dock master, William made many outstanding contributions to local and international maritime and seafaring life, all based on sound scientific principles. We still benefit from these visionary innovations today. Here are just a few:

1 One of the most important of Hutchinson's achievements was his production of the first accurate set of tidal and meteorological measurements in Britain. Between 1768 and 1793 he kept a register

of tides with which he could predict the times for opening the gates of Liverpool's Old Dock. This had first opened to shipping in 1715, the year of William's birth. His exceptionally accurate and detailed records led to the publishing of the first tide tables, which were in use almost as soon as they had been printed. These tables continue to form the basis of modern tide tables, and his work received national recognition.

2 In 1763, William designed and introduced parabolic mirrors for use in lighthouses. He had experimented for a number of years and had built a large mirror that was 12ft in diameter. This he had made up of smaller mirrors, set into plaster, inside a wooden bowl-shaped frame. He tested his mirror in the signal station that then stood at the top of Bidston Hill on the Wirral. His belief was that the reflection of a lighthouse lamp by a parabolic mirror would carry the beam further out to sea, and he was proved correct.

3 He influenced the revolutionary design of lighthouses at Hoylake and Leasowe, which were both fitted with his new mirrors. In 1771, a new lighthouse was constructed on Bidston Hill, and this was also fitted with a Hutchinson parabolic mirror. William's design was then replicated and fitted in lighthouses right around the coast of Britain. The number of seafarers' lives that have been saved as a result of his invention must run into tens of thousands.

4 In 1766, Liverpool Corporation acknowledged that William had been the inspiration for the establishment of what was, in effect, the first lifeboat station in the world. This was at Formby, where he was responsible for 'ordering the establishment of a boat, dedicated to the purpose of saving life from drowning, to be stationed overlooking the outer reaches of the port at Formby, financed by the Dock Committee'. In the same year, William created the Mersey Pilot Service for local waters and the Mersey Approaches, following the passing of the Liverpool Pilotage Act by Parliament, in 1766. The modern Pilot Service continues to provide ships sailing into the Mersey with highly skilled knowledge and experience of the river's treacherous channels and shifting sandbanks.

5   Hutchinson published his first book, *Treatise on Practical Seamanship*, in 1777. It was the first of four editions that told tales of his long and considerable experience at sea. From this expert perspective he offered advice and observations on seamanship, ship and crew management, and navigation. His book also included advice on methods of lifesaving. This was very much needed as, at that time, common lifesaving methods included bloodletting from the drowned person's body; draping it over a trotting horse; or blowing smoke into them through the anus using a pair of bellows! (This is the derivation of that well-known phrase expressing disbelief – 'don't blow smoke up my arse'!)

With his friend, Dr Thomas Houlston, senior physician at the Liverpool Infirmary, William had discovered that if pulled from the water quickly enough many people could be resuscitated by more practical methods than smoke-filled bellows! In fact, in the process of research for this project Hutchinson saved twenty-six people who had either fallen from the quays, or overboard from ships into Liverpool's docks and wharves.

6   In April 1778, at the age of 62, William took command of the Queen Anne's Battery in Liverpool. This defensive fort had been erected on the north shore, just up from the saltwater baths that had been built some years before. It was essentially a high, semi-circular wall facing onto the river, with embrasures for around a dozen large 18lb canon. This enclosed a large courtyard area with a brick wall on the landward side. The fort was ready to repel an expected assault on the port by the American revolutionary, John Paul Jones (1747–92). However, the attack never came. The battery was only taken down in 1817, to accommodate the building of the new Princes Dock.

7   William also directed the removal of a major hazard to shipping at the mouth of the Mersey. This involved the cutting away of a ridge of rock and gravel, and the deepening of the channel near Perch Rock at New Brighton. The new channel was named after him.

8   In 1794, William published another influential book with the wonderful title, *A treatise on naval architecture founded upon philosophical and rational principles: towards establishing fixed rules for the best form and proportional dimensions in length, breadth and depth, of merchants ships in general, and also the management of them to the greatest advantage, by practical seamanship, with important hints and remarks relating thereto, especially both for defence and attacks in war at sea, from long approved experience.*

William Hutchinson died on 7 February 1801, at the remarkable age of 85, and was buried in St Thomas' churchyard in Park Lane. In 2008, as part of the development of the Liverpool ONE retail and leisure complex, which sits directly over the former creek, pool and Old Dock of Liverpool, a memorial to Hutchinson was created. This takes the form of a long, inscribed pavement bordered by a series of water jets. These make an attractive fountain and water feature that marks the boundary of the Old Dock. The inscriptions are of the measurements of the heights and times of high water at the Old Dock that William took during January 1783.

The world, as well as Liverpool, certainly does owe a massive debt of gratitude to this formidable, energetic and visionary seafarer.

WILD TIGERS IN TRANMERE

In the early evening of 27 June 1939, Chapman's Travelling Zoo & Circus was performing in the car park of Tranmere Rovers Football Club, on the outskirts of Birkenhead on the Wirral. A fair-sized crowd of adults and children were outside the Big Top, standing close by and watching as the two tigers, Romeo and Bengal, were returning from their performance inside the huge circus tent. The large animals were slowly making their way through a long, low, narrow wire tunnel to their cage in the car park – there was no Health and Safety Executive in those days! But one of the circus hands was distracted for a few moments and did not see that the tunnel had an unexpected gap in it. The tigers simply walked through this and out into the car park, whilst the crowd of spectators now quickly scattered.

The tigers did not give chase; in fact, Bengal wandered casually through the open main entrance of the Big Top, which was still full of happy circus goers. Fortunately, just as members of the audience saw the great beast lope into their midst, and before a mass panic began, the big cat was quickly captured, removed from view and returned to his cage.

However, Romeo made his escape from the car park into Borough Road. He suddenly leapt through the hawthorn hedge in front of some of the houses and into their front gardens. The very large and powerful animal then simply lay down in the front garden of No. 749. Just as he was settling down for a snooze amongst the flowerbeds he was aroused when a police van arrived with its bells ringing. Circus hands speedily turned up too with a travelling cage, inside which was Bengal. This was in an attempt to lure the other tiger inside, but Romeo now quickly made his way into the adjoining gardens.

When he reached No. 745 an animal trainer managed to coax the tiger to go into an open garage on the property, quickly closing the doors on it as soon as it was safely inside. Fortunately, the tiger fell asleep on the garage floor almost immediately! This gave the police

Romeo and Bengal safely recaptured. (Discover Liverpool library)

time to position the one end of a, now secure, wire tunnel leading into the travelling cage outside the garage door, which was then carefully opened. Using a long pole the trainer now gently woke the slumbering animal, who roused himself and stood up. Romeo was then successfully coaxed into the tunnel and through to the cage, where he joined Bengal.

Both tigers were back in time for the evening performance, which went ahead as if nothing had happened!

LIVERPOOL'S GRIM GAOLS AND THE 'LONG DROP'

From the sixteenth century most of Liverpool's 'lost villages' each had their own 'bridewell' or 'lock-up'. These were used to incarcerate for short periods their drunkards, vagabonds, n'er-do-wells and petty miscreants. Only those in Everton and Wavertree survive. These had both been built in the eighteenth century, specifically to imprison people who had come to these delightful and picturesque communities as tourists, but who had enjoyed far too much of the local ales and had then made nuisances of themselves.

From the eighteenth century Liverpool town itself had small bridewells near the docks, to accommodate troublemaking seafarers and dock workers. However, it also had a larger town gaol in the cramped, airless and ill-lit dungeons and cells of the ancient Tower of Liverpool. This former riverside mansion had been fortified as a military garrison, in 1406, by Sir John Stanley (*c.* 1350–1414), and it stood at the bottom of Water Street. Conditions for prisoners here were so squalid that disease was rife; as was starvation, physical brutality and sexual abuse.

In 1774, and again the following year, the respected prison reformer John Howard (1726–90) visited all of the town's gaols and lock-ups as part of his national inspection of Britain's prisons. However, he was particularly appalled at the overcrowding and filth in the primitive Old Tower. Men, women and children were packed in together with no regard to age, gender or decency in cells often awash with urine, vomit and excrement. Howard insisted that this be closed as a gaol and replaced by a more civilised and wholesome establishment.

He also used Liverpool as a prime example of the desperate national need for drastic changes to be made in the whole attitude to the imprisonment and general treatment of criminals. The town Corporation were so embarrassed by his very public exposure of this scandal that they invested in the first 'modern' prison to be built in Liverpool. This was also the first purpose-built 'locally-administered penitentiary' in Britain. Even so, construction work did not begin until 1785, and it was erected on a street that the Corporation named after the reformer, Great Howard Street.

The new gaol was designed by London-born prison architect William Blackburne (1750–90), but with contributions by Howard. The building comprised six blocks of single-occupancy cells, which fanned out in a semi-circle from a central administration unit. The new gaol also pre-empted the government's Penitentiary Act of 1799 which, amongst other provisions, specified that gaols should be built with one cell per prisoner. The entire complex was enclosed behind a high wall with a single entrance directly from the street.

Although still unfinished, from 1793 and during the first twenty years of its existence, around 4,000 prisoners of war spent varying periods of time in the new Liverpool Borough Gaol. These were French soldiers and sailors captured during the Napoleonic Wars (1803–15) and, as a result, the building became known in the town as the 'French Prison'. Sadly, conditions here were not much better than those in the Tower. The gaol could be stifling in summer and freezing in winter.

Food was limited in quantity and very poor in quality. In fact, many inmates were forced to survive by eating rats, mice and larger insects. They also had to earn money to buy food from their jailers, by constructing and selling toys, trinkets and model ships and animals. These pieces of 'scrimshaw' were often intricately carved from bits of bone and scraps of wood, and were then sold to visiting members of the public. Some of these items survive in the Museum of Liverpool, and they are remarkably detailed and quite beautiful.

Townspeople were allowed to enter the prison for their own entertainment, rather like going to a zoo, providing they paid a few pence as a bribe to the jailers. The prisoners also put on concerts and performed plays for these 'tourists', receiving payment in money, food and smaller items of clothing.

Liverpool's local criminals, as well as incarcerated debtors, only began to be moved from the dungeons of the Tower and into the Borough Gaol from 1811. This was when the Frenchmen began to be released and repatriated, but thirty-six years had passed since Howard had condemned the medieval building!

The grisly Old Tower of Liverpool was eventually demolished in 1819, and modern Tower Buildings now stands on the site. However, as the population of Liverpool rapidly expanded throughout the nineteenth century, so did incidents of both petty and violent crime. Larger and more secure prisons were now required, because the old Borough Gaol could only accommodate a maximum of around 400 inmates at any one time. So, in 1819 a new prison was built at Kirkdale, just to the north of the town, on the road to Bootle. With single-occupancy cells, this stood near modern Kirkdale railway station and was one of the largest and most modern prisons in England at that time.

But demand *still* increased. So, in 1855, another and much larger prison was built at Walton, also to the north of the town centre. This also had single cells to accommodate an average of between 800 and 1,000 prisoners in five wings. Originally these were both male and female inmates housed in separate blocks.

By 1865, the old Borough Gaol on Great Howard Street had been demolished. Kirkdale itself closed in 1897, and its prisoners were transferred to nearby Walton, simply by marching them through the streets. Soon afterwards Kirkdale Prison was also demolished and its site is now a park and recreation ground.

What became known locally as 'Walton Jail' is now Her Majesty's Prison Liverpool, and is for male prisoners only. An entire wing was bombed during the Second World War and, although this was never rebuilt, the prison can accept up to 1,500 inmates. However, this is sometimes with three men in a cell originally designed for one person. The building is often filled to capacity and is currently the largest prison for men in Western Europe.

But, of course, prison terms were not the only punishments meted out to criminals. For the most serious crimes execution was the most likely sentence. Over the centuries, methods of judicial killing were beheading and pressing under stones and weights. For the worst

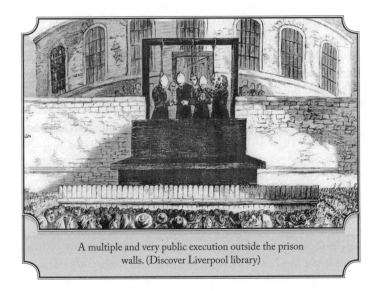

A multiple and very public execution outside the prison walls. (Discover Liverpool library)

crimes the grisly 'hanging, drawing and quartering' was used, but most common was the traditional method of hanging, from a beam or scaffold, which caused death by slow strangulation.

Many executions were carried out at both Kirkdale and Walton Prisons, and at Kirkdale these had been held in public. Condemned men and women were hanged on a scaffold erected outside the prison walls in front of often vast crowds. This was supposed to act as a deterrent but, in fact, it simply provided a thrilling entertainment and a chance for a day out for people for whom life was cheap anyway.

Special 'execution excursions' were organised, and carts and coaches full of people travelled the roads to the prison, whilst special ferryboat trips carried hundreds of river-borne spectators to Kirkdale. These vessels anchored close to the Mersey shore, opposite Kirkdale Prison, providing a grandstand view for the happy passengers. Men, women and children would excitedly chatter and gossip until the prisoner (and there was often more than one) was brought out and his head placed in the gallows noose. The trapdoor upon which the condemned prisoner stood was usually held closed by props beneath it. The executioner would then have to go below and knock these out of the way to release the drop. When the prisoner fell and the strangling began great cheers of delight would usually go up from those watching. This was unless the prisoner was popular with the people, when just as loud cries of distress and anger would result.

The last person to be hanged in public in Britain was Michael Barrett, who was executed on 26 May 1868. A militant Irish Republican, Barrett had placed a bomb in a wheelbarrow in a busy street in Clerkenwell in London. When this exploded it killed twelve innocent bystanders. There were no shouts of disapproval when he was hanged outside the walls of Newgate Prison.

It was in 1868, that the law was changed and executions no longer took place as a public spectacle. By this time, though, hanging had become the only official method of execution and the process was generally becoming much quicker and more efficient. This was because hanging now utilised a drop through a quick-release trapdoor that opened onto a deep pit. As the condemned person fell, his descent was sharply halted by the rope around his neck that was fixed to the gallows bar above. Also, the noose was now positioned in such a way that the bodyweight of the convict would then cause his neck to be snapped sharply. This was known as the 'long drop' and it resulted in an almost instantaneous and more humane death. That was providing the executioner was experienced and efficient, of course – there had been some unexpected decapitations!

Now, and in common with all other large British prisons of the time, Kirkdale and Walton both had 'execution sheds'. These were located well within the prison walls and away from the public. Both gaols shared a fully portable scaffold and gallows that was transported between them as necessary.

However, in 1885, the trapdoor failed to open on the gallows being used in Exeter Prison. Because of this, the Home Office commissioned Lieutenant Colonel Alton Beamish to design a more efficient, standard model of gallows and drop for permanent installation in all British prisons. This updated design consisted of two uprights, spanned by a length of oak beam measuring 8in square. This was long enough to execute three prisoners side by side, using a double trapdoor that was 12ft long by 4ft wide. An efficient lever and bolt mechanism now opened the hinged doors of the trap in one smooth action.

The first person to die in Britain using the new design of gallows was Matthew William Chadwick, at Kirkdale on 15 April 1890. Both of Liverpool's Victorian prisons saw many hangings between 1887 and 1964, when executions ended in Britain. In Walton Prison alone sixty-two people were executed during this period.

In 1892, a new execution chamber with an adjoining condemned cell had been constructed at Walton. This was made by connecting the last two cells on 'I' Wing and by using the cell immediately below as the hanging pit. Even though, after 1964, the execution area was converted back into ordinary cells again, part of the gallows beam can still be seen as a section of the internal wall. It is also said that the ghosts of some of the unfortunates hanged at Walton still haunt this part of the prison.

The last woman to be executed in Britain was the murderess, Ruth Ellis. Aged 29, she was hanged at Holloway Prison in London on 13 July 1955 at 9.01 a.m. She died at the hands of Britain's principal executioner at that time, Albert Pierrepoint (1905–92). By this time, the process of judicial killing had reached a peak of efficiency, particularly because of the skills of professionals like Pierrepoint. This meant that from the time Ellis walked into the execution chamber to the moment of her death only ten seconds passed.

The last executions to take place in Britain were of two male accomplices in a violent robbery and brutal murder, and their simultaneous hangings took place on Thursday, 13 August 1964. The names of the condemned men were Peter Anthony Allen, who was 21 years old, and Gwynne Owen Evans (AKA John Robson Walby, or Welaby), who was 24 years old. However, whilst they died at exactly the same time (8.00 a.m.), multiple executions had long since ended and so they were hanged in separate prisons. Evans died at Strangeways Prison in Manchester and Allen at Walton Prison.

On the day before his execution, Allen was visited by his wife. He suddenly threw himself violently against the glass that separated them and he slightly cut his wrists. But the following morning his execution went ahead nonetheless. As he entered the execution chamber at Walton he is said to have called out, 'Jesus!' when he saw the noose hanging from the gallows beam.

And so, on that August day in 1964, capital punishment and the 'long drop' ended in Britain. The Home Office decided that those condemned prisoners still awaiting execution in the country's jails should have their death sentences commuted. Even so, hanging remained a statutory penalty in British law for certain other offences, including treason, but it was never imposed. Judicial execution in the UK was finally, formally and completely abolished in 1998.

THE SMALLEST HOUSE IN ENGLAND

The district of Wavertree, to the south-east of Liverpool town centre, is another of the city's 'lost villages' that was once an independent township in its own right. Despite being swallowed up in 1895 by the rapidly expanding conurbation, Wavertree village retains many special features – if you know where to look. One of these is the former pub named the Lamb Hotel. Standing on High Street, the building dates from 1851, and is now the offices of a law firm.

The old and very large tavern stands on the site of an older inn that was referred to as early as 1745. The Lamb was built as a coaching inn but coaches never used it. Instead, a local entrepreneur by the name of William Dilworth ran horse-drawn omnibuses from here to the heart of Liverpool. He was a direct rival to Joseph Mattinson's horse trams, which ran from the older Coffee House Inn, just around the corner, and the competition between the two men was fierce.

Wavertree was already a popular day trip out from the town, because the village then nestled at the centre of Wavertree Green, surrounded by farms, copses and the rolling countryside of the Great Heath. There was also a large lake in the village, fed by a spring and an ancient well, where people came to swim. But it was its numerous taverns, inns and beer houses that made Wavertree particularly attractive to the vast majority of day trippers. As a result both coach companies thrived and were profitable for their respective owners.

In fact, the district had been a popular destination since the eighteenth century, when trippers from Liverpool first descended on Wavertree for the fairs held on the green. Morris dancers, bull and bearbaiting, cockfighting, boxing, wrestling and races were just some of the entertainments on offer.

One of the other pubs to which these early tourists flocked still operates just a few doors down from the Lamb. This is the Cock &

Bottle, which is also one of the oldest pubs in the village, although it was originally a temperance coffee house. It is actually two early eighteenth-century cottages that were knocked into one sometime in the nineteenth century. Recently fully refurbished, the pub is attractive both inside and out and serves excellent beers and home-cooked food. However, of particular significance is the fact that alongside the pub stands what was once the smallest house in England; and it clearly looks from the street like a miniature dwelling.

The smallest house in Britain is a title held by a sixteenth-century fisherman's cottage in Conway, in North Wales, but the Wavertree cottage was almost as small when it was built in 1850. This was in what had been a passage alongside the inn, and the little building was only 6ft wide and 14ft from front to back when it was completed.

It was given the address of No. 95 High Street and was created by another local enterprising opportunist, who took advantage of the fact that thousands of immigrants were now pouring into Liverpool, mostly from Ireland. These people were seeking work and were desperate for somewhere to live, even if it meant renting a former alleyway! The miniature house on High Street had a front door that opened onto a tiny ground floor room with a window to the street.

The smallest house in England in the 1890s …
(Liverpool Athenaeum library)

There was a staircase leading up to the first floor, which also had a window overlooking the street. There was also a fireplace, complete with a chimney and a pot on the roof.

There are stories of a couple raising eight children here and also of another very large resident, who had to go upstairs sideways. This was after the staircase had been widened to accommodate him – from its original width of 8in to 16in! The last inhabitants of the smallest house, Mr and Mrs Richard Greaves, moved out in 1925. The building then remained empty until 1952, when one of the side walls was knocked through and it became part of the Cock & Bottle pub lounge. In 1998, the owners of the pub restored the external appearance of the house, which can be clearly seen from outside the building.

... and today. (Discover Liverpool library)

Recently, the wall that originally separated the pub from the tiny dwelling was reinstated. Even so, its front door does not open onto a house but to a full-sized staircase that leads up to new apartments in the roof of the pub. Because it is no longer a self-contained home this curiosity cannot reclaim its previous title of the smallest house in England, but it still looks as if it could!

MILLER'S CASTLE AND THE NUDE BATHERS OF BOOTLE STRAND

Bootle is the town that stands immediately on the northern border of Liverpool, but it is very much part of the city and its people. Its name comes from the Old English word 'botl', meaning 'dwelling house'. Though very much part of the riverside conurbation today, it was once a quiet, pleasant village that was famous for fruit and vegetable farming, and it supplied the community for miles around.

During the eighteenth and nineteenth centuries, Bootle village became the home of many wealthy businessmen, from all over Liverpool and south Lancashire, who appreciated its rural peace and beauty. This helped Bootle to rapidly become a fashionable seaside resort, particularly because of its long stretches of golden beach and sandhills. At that time these still graced the shores of the River Mersey and attracted many hundreds of people each summer for their health and recreation.

Many people, especially young men and boys, but some girls and women too, also came up to the Bootle strand from Liverpool to go bathing and swimming in the river. Of course, they did not have bathing costumes, and would not have bothered to wear them even if they had; fun and frolic in the water, just as nature intended, was all they cared about. Unfortunately this flaunted nudity outraged the sensibilities, and the moral superiority, of the socially aspirational families now sauntering along the sands in their smart suits and crinoline gowns – and in front of their children and servants too! Something had to be done.

A local bylaw was passed to prevent nude sea bathing, but the demand was still there. This was when an enterprising Liverpool solicitor by the name of William Spurstow Miller, as a sideline, began

Miller's Castle and some of his bathing machines on the
Bootle strand. (Liverpool Athenaeum library)

to rent out bathing machines for the swimmers. These were like large
sheds mounted on cartwheels and with a door at each end. They had
high windows in them for light, air and discretion, and fully clothed
bathers entered these through the rear door and closed this behind
them.

Inside their cabins they would then get undressed, whilst horses or
strapping young men towed the contraptions out into the water. Then
the bathers would come out of the other door in the front of the boxes
to find a set of steps leading them discreetly below the water line. This
was at a safe paddling and swimming depth and it also covered their
nakedness. Even so, and for decency's sake, male bathers used a set of
machines located at one end of the beach whilst women used another
set positioned at the other end of the strand.

Miller also rented out the Victorian equivalent of sun loungers
and deck chairs for those people who did possess and wear bathing
suits. All of this proved so lucrative and popular that he increased his
already considerable wealth. So much so that, in 1824, he built a huge
crenellated mansion house for himself on the shoreline, and he named
it 'Miller's Castle'. He also built the local church, St Mary's, in 1826,
and paid for the laying out of the main road from Liverpool to Bootle
(and so leading people directly to his bathing machines!). He named
this Derby Road, in honour of Lord Derby who once owned the land
in the area.

By 1825, the Lancashire historian, Thomas Baines, was describing
the settlement at Bootle as a 'pleasant marine village … much resorted

to in the summer season as a sea-bathing place'. Now Bootle was also attracting those coming to 'take the waters', which had become the latest thing for the middle classes to indulge in. They came here from the town of Liverpool and surrounding districts, by cart and carriage and on foot, to stroll and relax with their families. They also came, quite purposefully, to drink the river water for its much promoted and alleged health-giving properties. The recommended treatment was '½ pint of milk mixed with ½ pint of Mersey water, imbibed 8 times a day'! Bootle was now an almost fashionable spa town.

Miller died in 1850, and his castle was demolished in the 1860s. This was to make way for the creation of the North Docks, and it was around the same time that the Dock Road was laid out, together with a road from there up to Walton. Named Miller's Bridge in tribute to the enterprising lawyer, this very busy main road now crosses over the Leeds–Liverpool Canal and the northern railway line.

Apart from his name, nothing now remains of Miller's Castle, his bathing machines, the beautiful beaches, nor of the nude bathers of Bootle!

'Stand and Deliver!'

> The wind was a torrent of darkness among the gusty trees,
> The moon was a ghostly galleon tossed upon cloudy seas,
> The road was a ribbon of moonlight over the purple moor,
> And the highwayman came riding-riding-riding
> The highwayman came riding, up to the old inn-door.

Alfred Noyes: *The Highwayman* (1907)

Travel, even between local areas, is quite a modern concept. People only began to move around the country from the time of the Industrial Revolution (*c.* 1760–*c.* 1830), and this only became commonplace as the twentieth century dawned. In the years before the English Civil Wars (1642–51) few ordinary people travelled beyond their own town or village, unless they were on official business for the State or the Lord of the Manor, or were going to a market or fair. Merchants also travelled around, though, to conduct business. However, most people lived, worked and died in the place where they were born, and never left it. In fact, until the mid-eighteenth century there were only a few roads connecting Britain's communities, which were mostly self-sufficient.

When people did need to travel they would do so on foot, unless they were wealthy enough to afford horses, carts or wagons. In and around Liverpool, especially to the east, all travellers would have to cross the Great Heath. This was a vast area of open moor, grass and scrubland, covering the area for miles around. Narrow, winding tracks crossed what was also known as 'the waste', leading to the nearest villages such as Childwall, Wavertree, Woolton or West Derby.

Travellers generally made their journeys during the day, because that was the only time they could actually see where they were going, and because it was safer – well, up to a point! Even though these were distances of only 3 or 4 miles they were vulnerable to attacks by 'footpads' who operated alone or in small gangs.

These were vicious thugs who would suddenly leap out from behind hillocks, large rocks or occasional copses or woodlands, terrifying isolated travellers. Footpads were ruthless and demanded goods, money and even the clothing of their victims. Failure to hand everything over quickly would certainly result in the footpad using his 'hanger' (short sword), or a great bludgeon, or perhaps his heavy, weighted cosh, to beat, maim, mutilate or kill. Indeed, the footpad and his henchmen would probably kill you anyway, leaving your naked corpse lying forlornly on the open heath.

But these villains did not always have it their own way. Sometimes the traveller would give as good, or better, than was being handed out! Sometimes too, the law would catch up with the robbers, when they would face the ultimate penalty for their crimes – the slow, strangled hanging at the end of a rope in front of baying crowds at their public execution.

By the closing decades of the 1600s, and before the development of canals, Liverpool was growing into an important mercantile centre. More and more goods and supplies were being transported in and around the town by road. It was cheaper and marginally safer to move goods this way, rather than by sea, although roads were no more than beaten footpaths, pack-horse trails or cart tracks, worn into place by centuries of use. Travel could be hazardous because even the main routes were seldom maintained, despite the fact that local parishes were legally obliged to do so. This meant that the roads became overgrown, strewn with rocks, rutted and uneven, or full of hollows and potholes – many quite deep. In bad weather these might fill with rainwater and many travellers might fall in and drown. Often, roads would be washed away in storms or rendered completely impassable.

But as travel became increasingly frequent and necessary, especially by the mid-1700s, most male travellers would journey on horseback, either alone or in small groups. Families travelled by cart, carriage or coach, if they could afford them, but women never travelled alone because this was considered indecent! Also, the mail was being transported around the countryside, and mail coaches and post boys were now targets for robbers. But these newer, faster forms of travel meant that the footpad was soon replaced by a much more sophisticated breed of roadway thief – the highwayman.

History paints a romantic portrait of these robbers, with Dick Turpin being the most famous, but in reality there was nothing romantic about them at all. On the loneliest stretches of road they would ride up to block the passage of a coach and brandishing a pistol – sometimes one in each hand – they would shout to the coachman, 'Halt, or I shall surely shoot!' For fear of his life the coachman would reign in the horses and the carriage would come to a stop. The highwayman might then fire a warning or a wounding shot. Next, he might actually demand, 'Stand and deliver! Your money or your life!' From the seventeenth century this phrase was in common use by such brigands on England's coaching roads.

With a distinct advantage over the footpad – that of being able to attack from a safe distance – the robber would force driver and passengers to hand over jewellery, money, silk handkerchiefs and any 'new-fangled' pocket watches. Once these were in the thief's possession he would use his other advantage of being able to make a fast getaway on horseback. But, as with the footpads, highwaymen did not have it all their own way.

As highway robberies became more prevalent on Liverpool's outlying roads, travellers began to carry their own pistols and swords, and coaches would often have armed escorts. Soon, highwaymen

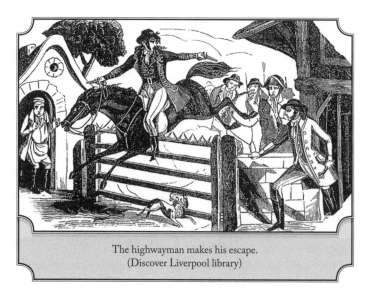

The highwayman makes his escape.
(Discover Liverpool library)

would find themselves captured and locked up, in small, purpose-built local gaols or bridewells. One such was in Old Swan village, where there was a tavern and stables at the junction of four principal roads at the heart of the Great Heath. But the Old Swan bridewell, which once stood at what is now the corner of Derby Lane and Prescot Road, was not well constructed. The large blocks of sandstone that made up its walls were not very well mortared, leaving narrow gaps between them. The roof and the iron door may have been secure, but the friends and associates of the captives would push the long, curved stems of clay 'churchwarden' pipes through the cracks. Placing the outside ends of these into bowls of wine or ale, and the inside ends between his lips, the prisoner could suck up as much drink as his friends could supply. This meant that a highwayman might be locked up completely sober yet be unlocked and taken to be hanged in a state of advanced drunkenness. Perhaps this made his slow strangulation less of an ordeal.

Highwaymen began to vanish from British roads by the early years of the nineteenth century; in fact, the last recorded robbery by a mounted highwayman took place in 1831. It was the development of better maintained, wider, turnpiked stagecoach roads with manned toll houses every few miles that eventually saw off these mounted robbers.

Now it was almost impossible for a highwayman to make a getaway without witnesses, or without lots of people to chase him to ground.

All we have now, in popular mythology, are tales of glamorous, masked and cloaked 'gentlemen thieves of the road', when actually these were dangerous, unscrupulous, violent thugs and murderers.

A CASBAH IN WEST DERBY

Liverpool is a small place, and yet one that has produced entertainers, musicians and artists of every kind. This means that almost everyone who lives there has some connection with someone famous, and they will tell of this whether you ask them to or not – and I am no exception!

During the late 1950s, my older brother (who was ten years my senior) for some time had been a member of a skiffle group. This style of popular music originated in America, and swept across Britain during the late 1950s. A blend of country, folk, blues and Dixieland jazz music, it was played on a small combination of basic instruments. Performed by such artists as Glasgow-born Lonnie Donegan (1931–2002), skiffle appealed to the new phenomenon, the 'teenager', especially in urban centres like post-war Liverpool.

This was because the instruments required to produce the sound were cheap and easy to acquire. My brother played one of the mainstays of any skiffle group, the washboard. He did so by placing thimbles on his finger-ends and then strumming these up and down the corrugated metal surface of this primitive washing machine. This provided rhythm as well as percussion. The rest of the group comprised a lad who played drums (usually a bass drum, a snare drum and possibly a crash cymbal as well); one or two other lads playing acoustic guitars; and one lad playing a tea chest double bass. This homemade musical instrument was an upturned empty wooden tea chest with a brush pole sticking up from one corner. A tight string ran from the top of the pole to the opposite corner of the chest, and when this string was plucked bass notes were produced.

My brother and his friends occasionally practised in the former coal cellar of a large, detached house at No. 8 Hayman's Green, in the

Liverpool suburb of West Derby. This building belonged to the mother of a young drummer, whose name was Pete Best (b. 1941). In 1959, the spacious basement of the fifteen room, mid-Victorian detached house had been converted into a private, members only coffee bar by Pete's extremely indulgent mother, whose name was Mona Best (1924–88). She was a formidable but affable woman who doted on her 17-year-old son. She also wanted to make sure that Pete had somewhere safe and atmospheric to bring his friends, and with whom he could play his drums.

Mona had bought the house in 1957, but had only been able to do so because, in 1954, she had pawned her jewellery and placed the cash on a horse running in the Epsom Derby that year. Ridden by a previously unknown jockey by the name of Lester Piggott (b. 1935), her horse won at odds of 33–1. The name of the horse was 'Never Say Die', and she adopted this as her family motto.

Mona Best. (Courtesy of Roag Best)

Mona called the cellar club the 'Casbah' and opening night was 29 August 1959. Around 300 teenagers from across Liverpool signed up as its first members that night, as they crowded into the West Derby basement. The club very quickly became an integral and famous part of the Merseybeat rock music scene of early 1960s Liverpool. The Casbah would also be one of two cellars in the city that would nurture and shape the global music scene, the other being the Cavern Club, of course.

To set high standards for her new enterprise Mona charged an annual membership fee of half a crown (25p), so that she could 'keep out the rough elements'. Very soon the membership of the Casbah had risen to 1,000 and amongst them were many teenage boys who would later go on to be members of some of the most famous rock and pop groups of that era. This combination of coffee bar, dance hall and youth club was carefully presided over by the ever watchful Mona. Even so, this did not stop the boys, and the girlfriends they brought with them, from having a great time. They drank tea, coffee from an espresso machine, or sometimes lemonade (or the occasional cider!), and they could also buy snacks and cakes. Then, those members who played instruments would jam together and so develop their musical and performance skills.

The first group to play at the Casbah was made up of four Liverpool lads who, in 1956, had formed themselves into the 'Quarrymen'. They called on Mona and asked her to book them, but the club wasn't finished yet. So they all helped her paint and decorate the cellar and its walls were soon covered with rainbows, stars, spiders and webs, and dragons. Most of this original artwork still adorns the walls of the Casbah today.

The names of the boys were John Lennon (1940–80), Paul McCartney (b. 1942), George Harrison (1943–2001) and Ken Brown (1940–2010). The girlfriend of John Lennon was then Cynthia Powell (1939–2015), and she painted a silhouette of her boyfriend on the wall of the new club, which is also still there. She went on to marry John and together they had a son, Julian Lennon, who was born in 1963.

The Quarrymen were all guitarists and they did not have a drummer at that time. Pete would go on to join them, though, and would be with the group when, in April 1960, they changed their name to the Beatles.

The Quarrymen perform on the opening night of the Casbah:
Paul McCartney sings as John Lennon carefully watches his
friend's guitar technique. (Courtesy of Roag Best)

They would already have been known as Johnny and the Moondogs, the Silver Beats and the Silver Beetles, by this time. The Quarrymen played the first seven consecutive Saturday nights at the Casbah and so became the club's first resident band. Before he joined the Quarrymen, Pete's own group, the Black Jacks, played there too.

In the autumn of 1960, the Beatles made their now legendary extended trip to Hamburg. Here, in the Reeperbahn, the red light district of Hamburg, they gave a season of gruelling but rapturously received performances at the Indra and Kaiserkeller Clubs. Then in December they returned to Liverpool and to the Casbah. Here, on 17 December, they played their first gig in Liverpool using their new name.

Other Liverpool groups and singers who performed at the club included the Remo Four, the Searchers, Rory Storm and the Hurricanes, Gerry and the Pacemakers and Cilla Black, and the Casbah went from strength to strength. However, Mona decided to close the club on 24 June 1962, and the Beatles became the last group ever to perform there.

In 2006, the long-closed former Casbah was awarded Grade II listed building status and a blue plaque by English Heritage. It was restored and refurbished, and reopened as a privately owned tourist attraction. This was around the same time that the National Trust restored and opened the former Liverpool homes of John Lennon and Paul McCartney to the public.

The Casbah has been fully equipped with modern facilities, and it can be booked as a performance and event venue. This is now one of the principal Beatles tourist attractions, and guided tours are available around this vital part of the history of the early Liverpool rock and pop scene. These tours are often led by Pete's young half-brother, Roag Best (b. 1962). His knowledge of the birth of the Merseybeat era and the Liverpool Sound is second to none.

Which now brings me to my own connection with the Casbah and the Quarrymen …

One weekend afternoon late in 1959, when I was almost 9 years old, my brother's skiffle group was to meet up with Pete Best at the Casbah. They planned to have a jam session with the Quarrymen, who were now playing a new sound called 'Rock and Roll'. Our mother had insisted that my brother had to 'take our Kenny with you, he's getting under my feet!' But he told her that the last thing that he wanted was to have this small boy hanging around 'cramping his style'. Nevertheless, and resentfully, he had to comply with her commands.

After taking the short bus ride from our family home in Broadgreen, and in mutually hostile silence, we arrived at West Derby. My brother did not want me with him and I did not want to be there either, as he larked around with his friends and they played their instruments together. I was left to my own completely ignored devices. But I soon became very bored, having to watch eight or nine big, greasy, pimply, leather-jacketed lads playing loud music, which I neither understood nor enjoyed.

During a break between songs I saw one of the guitarists sitting by himself in a corner. He was wearing a heavy black leather jacket with an upturned collar. He also wore a black shirt, dirty jeans and fashionable shoes, known as 'winkle pickers', which came to a point at the toes. His hair, like my brother's, was carefully sculpted into a quiff above his eyebrows and shaped into a point at the back of his neck. For obvious reasons this was known as a 'duck's arse' haircut. The whole ensemble was slicked securely into place having been lathered with a popular thick hair pomade named 'Brylcreem'.

The youth had a thin face and wore a hard expression. He was smoking a cigarette and staring disdainfully at me through slitted and smoke enshrouded eyes. It was almost as if he was issuing me with a challenge and I could not resist rising to it. Whilst my brother and the other lads were busy talking amongst themselves I walked over to the sullen teenager. I planted my feet slightly apart, placed my hands squarely on my hips, looked him directly in the eyes and told him, 'You can't play that guitar. You're rubbish you are!'

The boy said nothing. He simply leaned forward in his chair and slapped me hard across the face. Then he stood and walked over to join the others. Whilst the blow left a temporary impression on me, what was ultimately of greater impact is the fact that the boy who slapped me was John Lennon!

CHILDWALL VILLAGE AND ITS ABBEY

Childwall is one of Liverpool's south-eastern suburbs and, like so many of the modern city's outlying districts, was once an important township in its own right, existing centuries before Liverpool was founded, in 1207. Childwall also appears in the Domesday Book of 1086, whilst Liverpool does not, testifying to its historical significance. It was originally recorded as 'Cileuuelle', meaning 'a stream where youngsters meet', from the Old English words 'cild' and 'wella'.

At the centre of what is now quite a sprawling district sits the original heart of the village, through which runs the very ancient road known as Score Lane. This was once the main track that connected Childwall with Liverpool's other 'lost villages' – to the north, Broadgreen and Knotty Ash, and to the east, West Derby, and to Gateacre, Woolton, Garston and Speke in the south. It is in the vicinity of Score Lane that some of old Childwall's fascinating and important places and buildings survive.

These include All Saints Parish Church, which is the oldest church within the modern boundary of Liverpool city. Also, near to an area of delightful ancient woodland known as 'Childwall Woods and Fields', and past an eighteenth-century lodge house designed by the great architect John Nash (1752–1835), is the site of the now lost Childwall Hall. This had been built, in 1780, by Bamber Gascoigne Junior (1758–1824), Lord of the Manor of Childwall, MP for Liverpool and ancestor of today's Bamber Gascoigne (b. 1935), of *University Challenge* television fame.

The studios of the film and television company, Lime Pictures, now stand on the site of this stately mansion. Here *Brookside* and *Grange Hill* were produced, and *Hollyoaks* and many other programmes and films are created.

Just a little way along Score Lane from the church is an area of attractive landscaped parkland known as the Bloody Acre Field. It is believed that a particularly violent skirmish took place here around the time of the English Civil Wars (1642–51). This is likely to have been fought between the once staunchly Catholic people of Childwall and Puritan forces of Parliament. Opposite the church and on the corner of Score Lane and Childwall Abbey Road, stands the venerable and welcoming hostelry known as the Childwall Abbey Inn.

Nearby Childwall Abbey Road is a continuation of Childwall Priory Road, and the names 'Priory' and 'Abbey' would seem to indicate that there was once a significant religious house in the district but, in fact, no evidence for such a community exists. What can be established is that the 'priory' was actually an old farmhouse that once stood on the edge of the village. This was demolished in the 1930s, during the construction of a new road system, including the Queen's Drive ring road.

The name 'Abbey' may refer either to the architectural style of old Childwall Hall, or it might simply be a reference to the Monks of Stanlawe Abbey on the Wirral. These Cistercian monks once farmed land and bred livestock in the districts bordering Childwall during the twelfth and thirteenth centuries.

The Childwall Abbey has certainly been an inn since the early seventeenth century, and one of its doors dates from 1608; but this was not original to the building, having come from a farmhouse in nearby Allerton. The inn is a large, imposing rectangular structure, built of large blocks of sandstone. It has two floors and on either side of the front entrance two half-towers form bays that run the full height of the building. This all gives Childwall Abbey its medieval character, as do its windows, which are of a Gothic, almost broad lancet style, and its roof, which is crenellated.

Although it has been altered a number of times over the centuries, the origins of the pub are certainly medieval. Indeed, many archaeologists now believe that all or part of the present building was once the Chapel of St Thomas the Martyr, which dated from 1484. So, it may indeed have once had a religious function in local life. The pub is still a centre of community activity today and, as well as offering good food and ales, the Childwall Abbey Inn has also always provided accommodation. In fact, at the end of the nineteenth century and during the early years of the twentieth, the Abbey was popular with actors travelling to perform in Liverpool's many theatres. The renowned thespians, Henry Irving (1838–1905) and Ellen Terry (1847–1928), and the author of *Peter Pan*, J.M. Barrie (1860–1937), have all left their names scratched in the window of the upstairs room facing the Parish Church of All Saints and overlooking Childwall Valley and the rolling landscape beyond.

The Childwall Abbey Hotel. (Discover Liverpool library)

The Abbey has had some real characters as landlords over the years, and amongst its typically affable eighteenth-century innkeepers were in 1778, John Bibby, and in 1798, William Jackson. These hearty gentlemen welcomed travellers with blazing log fires, hearty home-cooked meals, fine ales and traditional Liverpudlian friendliness, good humour and conviviality.

Whilst Queen Victoria sat on the throne of Britain (1837–1901), amongst the renowned landlords of the Childwall Abbey Inn were John Rimmer and his wife, Jane. They were respected throughout the district and ran the inn with firm but sociable hands. Sadly, John Rimmer died prematurely and so for the next forty years the Abbey was run, just as formidably, by his widow.

Jane 'kept a good cellar and an orderly house', and would 'brook no unruly behaviour'. Indeed, if any suspicious or unsavoury characters tried to make use of the inn, or made a nuisance of themselves around the village, Jane would roll up her sleeves and be first in the line to 'box their ears and send them on their way'! In Jane Rimmer's time, games of quoits began to be played on a special pitch next to the inn, and Childwall became known for the skill of its players and for the intense local rivalry that the contests provoked. These games were played alongside equally hard-fought games of bowls, which have been a favourite sport on the green at the Abbey since the sixteenth century, if not earlier.

Childwall had always been a centre of fox hunting, and there have been riding stables behind the inn since the fifteenth century. This was also where the Earls of Derby and the Marquises of Salisbury, as well as other Lords of Childwall Manor who were all members of the Childwall Hunt, once kept kennels for their fox hounds. The stirrup cup would be taken outside the Abbey, before the hunt set off in pursuit of its quarry across the Great Heath that once spread out around the district.

Both John and Jane Rimmer presided over a special annual ceremony that took place in their tavern. Each year, at a formal dinner held in the Childwall Abbey Inn, a local worthy gentleman would be elected as a Freeman of Childwall. However, to qualify for this honour the candidate had to demonstrate that he was 'a free drinker, a free player, a thorough smoker, a jolly fox-hunter, and a dear lover of the female sex'!

However, outside the Childwall Abbey pub is also where a number of local people claim to have seen the ghostly figure of the 'Grey Lady of Childwall'. She appears to float a little above the roadway along Score Lane, but no one knows who she was, or why she haunts the village. Also, at the bar of the Abbey, you may hear tales of the dreaded 'Childwall Death Coach'. Perhaps you may even have the misfortune of seeing this terrifying spectre for yourself, depending on how much hospitality you have enjoyed in the Abbey.

This phantom made its first appearance in 1895, and is said to forewarn of impending doom. Preceded by an increasingly loud clatter of hooves and the rattling of traces and bridles, one next hears the scraping of wheels and the neighing of horses. Then suddenly there appears a large, black coach. Generally seen in the later hours of the night, but especially towards midnight, the coach is pulled by two panting and wildly galloping horses, each with glowing red eyes. On the driving seat sits a man dressed entirely in black, including his hat, and his great black cape swirls about him. As he cracks his whip to drive on the horses, one can see that his eyes glow red too, and the rictus grin on his skeletal face clearly shows him to be a denizen of hell.

At breakneck speed the coach comes up the hill from Childwall Valley beyond the church graveyard. It then tears across the Bloody Acre Field, veers along Score Lane past the Abbey Inn, and then it screeches around up Childwall Abbey Road and towards Childwall Priory Road. Here it slowly vanishes as it approaches what was once the Great Heath. But not before it is said to have snatched the wicked from their beds and from the streets, to carry them off to perdition.

But then, it is amazing what strange sights and curious happenings can be seen after a few good pints at the Childwall Abbey Inn …

THE BODY IN THE DERBY SQUARE DUNGEON

On Derby Square in Liverpool, at the top of Lord Street and adjacent to Castle Street, stands the great memorial statue of Queen Victoria. She dominates the square as she gazes implacably down Lord Street. The monument was erected in 1902 as a tribute to Her Majesty, who died in 1901.

Until 1897 the square was occupied by St George's Church. Built in 1734, with its tall and elegant spire, this was described at the time as being 'one of the handsomest in the kingdom'. This was the official church for the mayor and Corporation of Liverpool but, in 1863, the incumbent vicar gave a virulent anti-semitic sermon denouncing the choice of a new Jewish mayor for the town. To their great credit the entire congregation immediately stood up and marched out of the building. They made their way down Church Street and into St Peter's Church. They declared that this would then be the official Corporation place of worship.

But, before any of this, the site on the summit of the sandstone promontory that looked out over the Mersey was occupied by Liverpool Castle. This was built sometime around 1235, and was not finally demolished and removed until 1721. This was originally a formidable and grim bastion, constructed to defend what was then the new port and town of 'Leverpul'.

At three of the castle's corners stood great round, tall, crenellated towers. At its fourth, and facing onto Castle Street, was a great barbican tower. This had a portcullised entrance over a drawbridge across the deep, wide, water-filled moat that surrounded the entire structure.

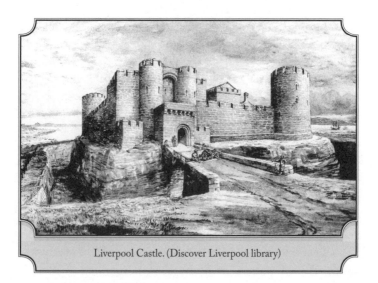

Liverpool Castle. (Discover Liverpool library)

As well as comfortable accommodations for the constable of the castle and his family, there were armouries, garrisons, a well, a forge, a bakery, an orchard, a dovecot, stables, a chapel, a great hall and all the other resources such a stronghold needed. It also had its places of torture and incarceration. In particular, deep below the castle were two large, lightless dungeons. There were also twenty-five cells, each only 6ft by 3ft square. This now brings us to a very sad and grim modern discovery.

In the early 1980s, as Derby Square was being excavated for the building of the Queen Elizabeth II Law Courts, the remnants of some of these ancient dungeons were exposed. In one of these was found the dried and perfectly preserved corpse of a uniformed Roundhead soldier. Had the poor man been incarcerated during the English Civil Wars (1642–51), when Liverpool and its castle changed hands three times between opposing forces? Had the trooper simply been forgotten and so left to starve to death? We are unlikely ever to find out. Who knows what other grisly finds may yet be discovered as more of ancient Liverpool is unearthed as the city continues its structural regeneration?

The site of Liverpool Castle today, and where the mummified body was found. (Discover Liverpool library)

NOVA SCOTIA, MANN ISLAND AND 'DICKEY SAMS'

In the eighteenth and nineteenth centuries, the area of Liverpool that is now the large shopping and leisure complex known as Liverpool ONE was once the place where the world's first enclosed, commercial wet dock had been built, in 1715. At that time this district was known as Sailor Town, because of the large number of seafarers who frequented the many brothels, taverns and lodging houses that could be found around the docksides. The whole area was then a warren of narrow alleys and streets, weaving between storehouses and other dockside buildings.

A six-lane highway known as the Strand now separates Liverpool ONE from the modern waterfront. Here, overlooking the river, stand the massive Albert Dock warehouse complex and the Maritime and Slavery Museums. Here, too, are the docks that surround these, as well as the four magnificent structures known as George's Dock Building and the Three Graces. The George's Dock Building is the headquarters for the Mersey Tunnels. Incorporated into this is a huge ventilation shaft for the Queensway Road Tunnel under the Mersey, connecting Liverpool and Birkenhead.

The Three Graces are actually the Port of Liverpool Building, the Cunard Building and the Royal Liver Building. When they were first collectively named as 'the Graces' is unclear, but this name was originally given to three of the daughters of the Greek God Zeus – Aglaia, who represented splendour and beauty; Euphrosyne, representing joy and festivity; and Thalia, representing abundance and good cheer. These buildings now form the most famous part of the Liverpool waterfront landscape and are recognised the world over. Interestingly, they all sit above the original George's Dock, and water still flows beneath them all.

The road that leads down to the river from the Strand, alongside George's Dock Building and the Port of Liverpool Building, is known as Mann Island. This name includes the area of land between this road and the docks of the Maritime Museum. However, at one time all of this actually was an island of sorts, and it has an interesting history.

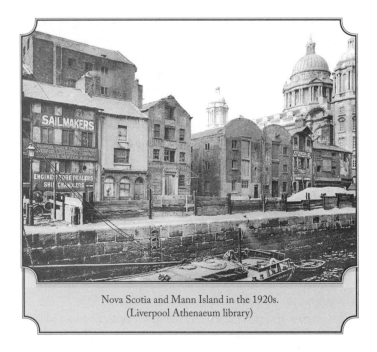

Nova Scotia and Mann Island in the 1920s.
(Liverpool Athenaeum library)

Before acquiring its Mann Island name and during the early eighteenth century, this section of the waterfront, which covers an area of no more than a few hundred yards, was first known as Nova Scotia. This was because of the number of seafarers and merchants who either sailed to, or traded with Nova Scotia in the New World, from this section of the riverfront. Over the years lodging houses, cottages, shops, taverns, small warehouses and manufactories appeared here, and a thriving if tiny community made Liverpool's Nova Scotia its home.

However, in 1767, work began on constructing George's Dock at a time when a merchant named John Mann lived and traded on Nova Scotia as an oil stone dealer and walking stick maker. He bragged continuously to his friends and neighbours that he would soon be living on an island. In fact, when the dock opened, in 1771, the small community did become surrounded by water on three sides – by the river to the west and docks to the north and south.

Soon afterwards, John's prediction was fulfilled when a canal was cut to the east of Nova Scotia linking the new dock with Canning

Dock and Manchester Dock (since filled in). Known as George's Dock Passage, this became part of the internal waterway that connects all of Liverpool's docks, making the entire system unique. John was now indeed entirely surrounded by water, and Nova Scotia soon acquired, light-heartedly, the new name of 'Mann's Island'.

John Mann died in 1784, but the name stuck (minus the 's') and the town Corporation decided to officially adopt the name for the area. George's Dock was closed, in 1900, and the Three Graces were soon built on the site, making Mann Island an island no more. All the buildings, taverns, cottages and workshops were eventually swept away. Standing there today are three stark, rectangular office blocks, encased in black glass panels and nicknamed 'the coffins', as well as the impressive Museum of Liverpool.

Liverpudlians are known as 'Scousers', after our dish and our dialect. More rarely we are referred to as 'Wackers', because we readily 'wack out' or 'share' things with each other. During the days of the wooden sailing ships, though, we were once known as 'Dickey Sams'.

The origins of this term are confusing, but some possible sources are these. In the eighteenth century, alongside George's Dock Passage on Mann Island, once stood a tavern known as Dickey Sam's. This was named after its landlord and owner, a certain Richard Samuel. Sailors often temporarily 'jumped ship' as their vessels made their slow progress through the 'cut', so as to have one last drink before sailing on to the river and the open sea. From that time, anyone living or who had been born on Mann Island (as many people were) was referred to as being a 'Dickey Sam'.

Alternatively, the name might have come from a small peaked woollen cap worn on board ship that was bought from a ship's chandlers on Mann Island. This store stood near the Dickey Sam tavern and the caps were quite popular. So anyone wearing one (including the ships' stokers carved into the *Titanic* memorial obelisk at the Pier Head) thus became known as a 'Dickey Sam'.

Another story tells how, on one of their frequent assaults on the port, the press gang once targeted the hapless sailors and male residents of Mann Island. This was to forcibly abduct them into long and often brutal service aboard the warships of the British Navy. Once all the men had been rounded up ready to be shipped out to sea, their names had to be taken down by the leader of the press gang. When asked for his name, the first man in the line said, 'Dickey Sam!' As did the second, third and fourth men, all the way down the line. The Scousers were about to be severely whipped for their typical Liverpudlian witty defiance, when the commanding officer simply said that everyone on Mann Island was a Dickey Sam, and ordered that they should all be listed as such on the official recruitment record!

Dickey Sams are also said to be those people who are born within the sound of the bells of Our Lady and Saint Nicholas Church, the 'sailors' church', which stands at the bottom of Chapel Street, overlooking the Pier Head and Mann Island.

Whichever of these explanations is true, the term is largely obsolete and Liverpudlians are most frequently also known as Scousers; an appellation I am more than happy and proud to accept for myself.

EASTHAM FERRY PLEASURE GARDENS

Eastham is quite an ancient Wirral village, nestling on the banks of the Mersey halfway down the Wirral Peninsula and overlooking south Liverpool. From the beginning of the nineteenth century, though, Eastham suddenly took on an important new role as a transport junction for those making journeys between Liverpool and Chester. This was in the days before the railways and better road communications.

Before this time, to get to Chester from Liverpool travellers had to take the ferry to Birkenhead at Woodside. Then there would be a long and uncomfortable coach journey, on a very poor and often unsafe road, all the way down the Wirral to the ancient Roman city. But, in 1815, a new steam ferry opened from Liverpool directly to Eastham, cutting the journey time considerably.

It had been the monks of Chester Abbey who first began a ferry service from Eastham to Liverpool, possible as early as the twelfth century. This was mentioned in the Domesday Book and, by 1509, it was known as Job's Ferry, and later as Carlett's Ferry. This was powered by a combination of sail and rowing and, depending on the river conditions, it could take hours to get across the Mersey.

In 1816, the very fast (for the times) paddle steamer, *Princess Charlotte*, was brought into service. This cut travel time even more. The Eastham Steam Ferry was a lucrative source of income for its owner, Sir William Massey Stanley (1807–63), who also owned a large estate of land surrounding the ferry landing point. However, the importance of the ferry route across the Mersey began to decline in 1833, when the renowned civil engineer, Thomas Brassey (1805–70), opened his New Chester Road from Birkenhead to Chester. This was well constructed and maintained, which meant that with a fast stagecoach the journey to Chester was much quicker than travelling via the Eastham ferry.

When, in 1840, the Chester to Birkenhead Railway opened, this provided an even quicker journey time, so business for the ferry declined even further. Because of this, and in a bid to replace lost revenue, in 1846 Sir William built the luxurious Eastham Ferry Hotel close to his ferry pier. This replaced a much less impressive older building. Stanley believed that this would encourage new visitors to Eastham, either by coach or ferry, but it was not enough. So, the following year he finally sold the estate, ferry and hotel to Richard Naylor, a Liverpool merchant. The new owner decided to develop Eastham as a pleasure garden to revive the fortunes of the ferry and his new property.

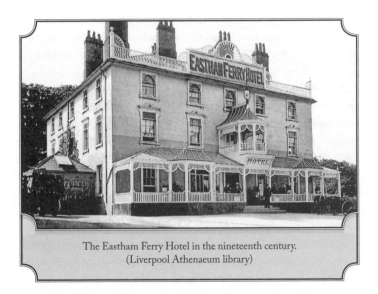

The Eastham Ferry Hotel in the nineteenth century.
(Liverpool Athenaeum library)

Naylor built a fairground and planted extensive flower gardens, including rhododendron walks and ornamental trees. There were also fountains and secluded glades for private canoodling and troth-plighting! He also provided band concerts, hobby horses and a water chute. The investment paid off and the gardens became very popular and highly profitable. In 1874, a new iron pier was built for the ferry boats, and by this time Eastham had become known as the 'Richmond of the Mersey' (after the town by the Thames).

Famous performers and entertainers appeared at the Eastham Ferry Gardens, including Charles Blondin (Jean François Gravelet, 1824–97), the famous Niagara Falls tightrope walker. He was 60 years old when he came to the pleasure gardens for a three-week engagement at Easter in 1884, and he insisted on performing his death-defying feats 75ft above the ground, even though a very strong wind was blowing. The crowds below the high wire on which he was precariously balanced pleaded with him to 'Come down sir! Come down, in the name of God!' Blondin simply ignored them, stood upright, blindfolded himself and put a sack over his head. Even though the wind had now become a gale he completed his walk without incident to the enthusiastic cheers and applause of the relieved spectators.

There was also a large menagerie and zoological garden in the pleasure grounds with a bear pit, lions, tigers, antelopes, seals, a monkey house and an aviary. Many people had never seen anything like this before, and one middle-aged man was seen fleeing from the zoo screaming in terror at the sight of the exotic and frightening creatures. Interestingly, George Mottershead (1894–1978), who founded Chester Zoo in the 1930s, is said to have witnessed a keeper's cruelty to an elephant in the Ferry Gardens Zoo which made him determined to ensure that the welfare of his own animals would be his top priority at his own new zoo.

Entrance to the gardens cost 3d and this gave access to all the entertainments. To get into the grounds visitors had to pass underneath the Jubilee Arch. This ornate structure had originally been erected in London Road, Liverpool, for Queen Victoria's visit to the city in her jubilee year of 1897. Once the arch had served its purpose it was sold at a knockdown price to the then owners of the gardens, where it became their formal gateway and ticket office.

The 'Flip-Flap' or 'Topsy-Turvy Railway' ride at Eastham Ferry Gardens. (Liverpool Athenaeum library)

Eastham attracted thousands of visitors from Liverpool and the Wirral every week. In fact, during 1908 alone 111,202 people visited the gardens. There was now also Fred Brooks' Vaudeville & Circus Co., a Pierrot theatre, a large ballroom, sideshows, tea rooms, an open-air stage and a boating lake; so there was something for everyone.

In 1909, the first 'loop-the-loop' rollercoaster ride in Britain transferred from Crystal Palace in London to Eastham. Known as the 'Flip-Flap' or the 'Topsy-Turvy Railway', this could reach an estimated speed of 95mph. However, it proved too scary for the public and stood idle for many years before being demolished.

Unfortunately the popularity of the pleasure grounds became its downfall and they became seen as somewhat 'common and not for families'. Visitor numbers declined and, in 1925, the ferry service was discontinued. Now with very few visitors, in 1929, Eastham Ferry Gardens were closed and, in 1935, the ferry pier was dismantled. When this service ended it also marked the end of paddle steamers on the Mersey.

The site of the old gardens is now Eastham Country Park. The Eastham Ferry Hotel still services visitors and with pleasant walks through the woods, excellent views across the river, and the fascinating remnants and relics from the old Ferry Gardens, this is still a popular destination for Merseysiders.

The Chinatown *Paifong*

The first significant numbers of Chinese immigrants arrived in Liverpool in the 1850s, which led to the city once being home to the largest and oldest Chinese community outside mainland China. Because of this, Liverpool and Merseyside have well-established and friendly links with that country. In fact, Liverpool was officially twinned with the city of Shanghai in 2000.

In that year, and as symbol of this friendship, a beautiful Chinese arch was erected at the top of Nelson Street, acting as a welcoming gateway into Liverpool's still sizeable and thriving Chinatown. Currently, there are more than 10,000 Chinese people living in and around Liverpool, and many new apartments, homes, shops and other amenities are being built on previously derelict land in the neighbourhood. This will considerably increase the size of Chinatown, which may also soon qualify for its own railway station.

The arch, or '*Paifong*', stands at a height of 44ft (almost 14m) and is the largest arch of its kind outside China; Liverpudlians of all races are very proud of it. Built in Shanghai of wood and marble at a cost of £700,000, the spectacular structure was designed by Mr Zhang of the South Linyi Garden Building Company, and built by their highly skilled artists and craftsmen. It was then dismantled and shipped to Liverpool, where it was reassembled by eight Shanghai painters, carvers and engineers. They worked every day for three months and only took three days off during this time.

Protected by two large bronze lions, the site for the arch was carefully selected by Feng Shui masters to ensure good fortune to the local community. As well as its five rooves and many other design features there are 200 dragons carved into the arch. Twelve of these are pregnant, which is considered a sign of good fortune. This combination of art and architecture is painted in five primary colours, each of which represents one of the five elements of Chinese mythology. These are:

Yellow – Earth   White – Metal   Red – Fire
Green – Wood   Black – Water

The Chinatown Arch, or *Paifong*. (Discover Liverpool library)

In the centre of the huge central span is a plaque on which are written Chinese characters that read (from right to left, naturally) '*Zhong Guo Cheng*'. These translate as 'Chinatown' or, to the Chinese, 'Middle Kingdom'. From around 1000 BC that was the name that the Chinese gave themselves. This was a time when the ancient people of the central plains of China believed that they were at the centre of the earth. They also believed they were the only true civilisation completely surrounded by a world of barbarians, therefore they were midway between earthly ignorance and the enlightenment of paradise – hence 'Middle Kingdom'.

Despite what it says on the *Paifong*, Liverpool's modern Chinatown is just one of many cultural and ethnic communities that make up this outstandingly diverse Capital of Culture. Unless, of course, one takes the view that the arch is a symbol of the fact that Liverpool and Merseyside are, in fact, the real 'Middle Kingdom'!

'WOMEN AND CHILDREN FIRST!'

On 30 December 1845, HMS *Birkenhead* was launched by the Marchioness of Westminster from the John Laird shipyard, in the town on the Mersey after which she had been named. This steam frigate was driven by two 20ft (6m) diameter paddle wheels and with two masts rigged as a brig. Commissioned by the Royal Navy as a troopship, she was one of the first iron-hulled ships.

After a number of years' service, on 25 February 1852, as well as a number of cavalry horses, *Birkenhead* was carrying ordinary soldiers and a number of officers with seven of their wives and thirteen children. Although some reports say around twenty-five women and thirty children sailed with the soldiers, the muster rolls of the vessel were lost so exact numbers are unknown. However, it is estimated that there were around 645 people on board.

Birkenhead was taking the men to fight in the 8th Xhosa War in South Africa and had set sail from Simon's Bay, near Cape Town, at around 6 p.m. in the evening. She was bound for Algoa Bay at Danger Point near Gansbaai; a voyage of around 87 miles (140 kilometres). Little did those on board suspect that the name of their destination was an ominous indication of what lay ahead for them.

Under the command of Captain Robert Salmond RN, who wanted to make the best possible speed, the ship kept within around 3 miles (4½ kilometres) of the coastline. With both her paddle wheels at full stretch she made an average speed of 8½ knots (15½ km/h). The evening passed into nighttime, the sea was calm and the sky was clear.

Just before 2 a.m. on the morning of 26 February, *Birkenhead* struck an uncharted rock just off Danger Point. No one saw it because it lies just below the surface. In calm waters, as on that morning, it remains hidden and is only exposed and visible in rough seas. The captain immediately ordered the anchor to be dropped, the paddles to turn astern and the lifeboats to be lowered. Predictably, there were not enough boats on board for the number of people; two were unserviceable and the winches had been painted over on the third. This left only two cutters and a small gig.

Tragically, the collision had made a great hole in the prow and as she backed off the rock the sea rushed into the front of the ship. Around ten minutes later the ship drove onto the rock again, which now tore the bulkheads apart and buckled the iron plates. Immediately, the forward compartments and the engine room were flooded and over 100 soldiers were drowned where they lay asleep in their berths.

The surviving soldiers mustered on deck and the women and children joined them, all standing at the stern in an attempt to raise the prow of the ship out of the water. Meanwhile, sixty men were assigned to operate the pumps and others assigned to the boats. The rest of the men stood completely silent on deck, maintaining military discipline and waiting for orders. The cavalry horses were untethered and driven over the side into the sea in the hope they would be able to swim to shore.

It was at this point that the ship appears to have split completely in two, aft of the mainmast. The funnel crashed into the sea and the forward part of *Birkenhead* sank right away, taking many men with it. The stern section, now crowded with men, stayed afloat for some minutes before it too began to sink. A survivor later reported, 'Almost everybody kept silent, indeed nothing was heard, but the kicking of the horses and the orders of Salmond, all given in a clear firm voice'.

Just before the rest of the ship began to sink Salmond called out, loudly but calmly, 'All those who can swim jump overboard, and make for the boats'. However, recognising that rushing the lifeboats would risk swamping them, the men were then ordered to 'stand fast' to allow 'the women and children to board first'. The men did indeed stand firm, except those who helped the women and children into one of the cutters, which had been positioned alongside. Only then were the men allowed to board the other two small boats whilst the rest simply abandoned ship. They had no alternative, because at that point the rest of the ship went down. One of the two boats was immediately swamped and the men were thrown into the sea. The third boat managed to get away safely, however. It had only been twenty minutes since *Birkenhead* had first collided with the Danger Point rock.

The following day, the schooner *Lioness* came upon the cutter with the women and children aboard and rescued them. They then successfully searched for the second boat and managed to save all the

The wreck of HMS *Birkenhead*.
(Discover Liverpool library)

men aboard that as well. She then sailed to the site of the wreck and saved as many of those still alive in the sea as possible. Some of the men had managed to swim the 2 miles to shore, although this had taken them around twelve hours. Others had clung to wreckage. But of those that went into the water and did not drown, many were eaten by the hundreds of sharks that had been drawn to the wreck and the thrashing of so many bodies in the sea.

Eight horses made it safely to land, but of the 645 people on board *Birkenhead* only 193 survived the wreck and the sea. The most senior officer to survive was Captain Edward W.C. Wright of the 91st Argyllshire Regiment. He later reported:

The order and regularity that prevailed on board, from the moment the ship struck till she totally disappeared, far exceeded anything that I had thought could be effected by the best discipline; and it is the more to be wondered at seeing that most of the soldiers were but a short time in the service.

Everyone did as he was directed and there was not a murmur or cry amongst them until the ship made her final plunge – all received their orders and carried them out as if they were embarking instead of going to the bottom – I never saw any embarkation conducted with so little noise or confusion.

The courage and chivalry of the soldiers became an illustrious part of the history of the sea. As did the fact that this was the first time that the 'women and children first' order had ever been issued. This became known as the 'Birkenhead Drill', and as a result it became the standard protocol during the evacuation of sinking ships.

The people of Birkenhead can be proud that the name of their town is now synonymous with courage and honour in times of fear and despair.

THE CATHEDRAL THAT NEVER WAS

Liverpool's great Anglican cathedral dominates one end of Hope Street in the city, and its foundation stone was laid by King Edward VII (1841–1910) in 1904. The Roman Catholic archdiocese also sought to demonstrate their faith in just as grand an architectural way. They had planned to do so in the mid-nineteenth century, but things had not gone to plan.

During the Great Irish Potato Famine (1845–52), 300,000 Irish men, women and children came to Liverpool to make the town their new home. They were escaping from exploitation, poverty, and starvation, and they swelled the Catholic population of the town dramatically. Because of this, the Catholic Bishop of Liverpool, Alexander Goss (1814–72), saw the need for a cathedral. He chose the grounds of St Edward's College on St Domingo Road in Everton as the site and, in 1853, awarded the commission to Edward Welby Pugin (1833–1875).

By 1856, the Lady Chapel of the new cathedral had been completed. However, because a great deal of money was now needed for the education of Catholic children, work on the building was not continued. The Lady Chapel was named the Church of Our Lady Immaculate, and it became the local parish church until it was demolished in the 1980s.

However, in the 1920s, and as the Anglican cathedral was slowly rising above St James's Mount, the archdiocese came up with a new plan for their own magnificent structure. The site eventually selected for this, on Mount Pleasant, by this time had achieved something of a tainted reputation. This was because, from 1771, it had been the location of one of the most notorious workhouses in Europe, the Liverpool Parish Workhouse. This had expanded over the years and the extensive complex of buildings covered an area of 9 acres, and was the unpleasant home to 4,000 desperate and destitute people. But, by the early years of the twentieth century, the workhouse had changed to providing care for the sick, the poor and elderly people. Then, in 1928, the revision of the Poor Laws closed the workhouse and brought the property onto the market in 1930.

The Roman Catholic archdiocese bought the complete site for £100,000, and Sir Edwin Lutyens (1869–1944) was commissioned as the architect for the new cathedral. By this time, Lutyens had already established an excellent international reputation because of his building of New Delhi from 1912–31, and, in 1919, for his design for the Cenotaph in London.

The site of the old workhouse was cleared and on Whit Monday, 5 June 1933, the foundation stone was laid. At the recommendation of Pope Pius XI (1857–1939), the cathedral was dedicated to Christ the King, and Lutyens' original design was for a huge Byzantine-style edifice. This was deliberately in direct contrast to the Gothic style of the Anglican cathedral.

The building would be constructed in pinkish brown brick relieved by bands of silver grey granite, and would be a massive 680ft long. The breathtaking structure would be crowned with an enormous dome, 168ft in diameter and 300ft high, taking the total height to 510ft. This would make the building the tallest cathedral in the country. It would also be 60ft higher than St Peter's Basilica in Rome, and more than twice the height of St Paul's in London (at 250ft).

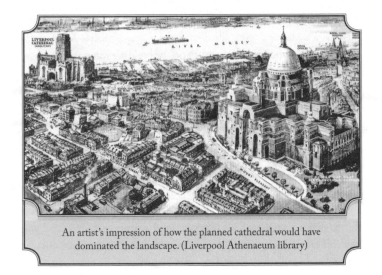

An artist's impression of how the planned cathedral would have dominated the landscape. (Liverpool Athenaeum library)

The high altar would have been 12ft above the base of the chancel, and fifty-three side altars would be located down the nave, along the aisles and in the transepts and apse. The entrance arch on the west portal would have been big enough to take the Victoria Clock Tower of Liverpool University. The new cathedral's height would tower over the nearby Anglican cathedral, itself 330ft tall; but perhaps that was the point.

In 1933, construction work began with the magnificent crypt. Designed, like the main cathedral, to be spacious and have a mystical grandeur. It was built in brick and granite quarried at Penryn in Cornwall. Work was progressing well, but then the archdiocese was to be thwarted once again.

In 1941, the financial and other restrictions of the Second World War, which was then at its height, forced the Catholic Church to stop the project. The estimated cost for completion had just risen from the original £3 million to £27 million (£1.17 billion at the time of writing). However, following the war, in 1956, it was agreed that work should continue on the crypt, which was then completed in 1958. Then, in a repeat of what had happened to this cathedral's predecessor, the rest of Lutyens' design was also abandoned. Instead, and with a very much reduced budget, a competition was held to find a new design and a new architect. This was won by Sir Frederick Gibberd (1908–84). Construction began in October 1962, directly above Lutyens' crypt, which was incorporated into the new design. Less than five years later, on the Feast of Pentecost, 14 May 1967, the completed Metropolitan Cathedral of Christ the King was consecrated.

To show us exactly what this colossal confection would have looked like, fortunately Lutyens' original architect's scale model survives. Between 1992 and 2005, conservators at the National Conservation Centre in Liverpool restored the wood, plaster and metal model at a cost of £500,000. At 11ft 9in wide, 17ft long and 12ft 6in high, the impressive model is on display in the Museum of Liverpool, at Mann Island.

JUDAS BURNING

One of the principal roads leading south out of Liverpool is Park Road, which runs over the high hill of Toxteth Ridge and was, originally, the 'road to the park'. This was the vast 3,000 acre Royal Toxteth Deer Park of King John (1167–1216), who had founded Liverpool in 1207.

The Deer Park was formally closed as such in 1592, and the first disafforestation began around 1596, when the clearing of the trees was started and the land was split up into farms. From that time 'the Park Road', as it then became known, ran through areas of open heathland and isolated rural communities, including the Dingle.

But with the coming of the Industrial Revolution (c. 1760–c. 1830) there was mass migration into Liverpool as people left the countryside to seek work in the rapidly expanding conurbation. All of what had then become the districts of Toxteth and Dingle soon became densely populated with tens of thousands of people, living in ranks of terraced, back-to-back and court dwellings that were then being built. Park Road became the main route in and out of the town for these new residents.

At the top of the hill on Park Road are four streets – Moses, Isaac, David and Joseph Streets, known collectively as the 'Holy Land'. These streets of terraced houses became a particularly close community, which is so typical in the working-class districts of Liverpool. However, the

Holy Land had its own peculiar, unique, annual Easter custom, which was known as 'Judas Burning'.

In the run up to Easter, children aged between 8 and 12 years old, and only from this neighbourhood, would go round the local shops and houses collecting wood for a bonfire. Each street or rival gang in the Holy Land would also make an effigy, rather like a Guy Fawkes. In this case, however, these represented Judas Iscariot, the disciple who betrayed Jesus Christ to the Romans and Jewish leaders, and which ultimately led to Christ's trial and crucifixion. These effigies were built with great care and pride, and each gang would try to steal each other's Judas.

Then, and again just in the four streets of the Holy Land, all of the Judases would be paraded around, accompanied by cries of 'A penny for Judas's breakfast'. At the same time the rival groups of children, watched by the other residents of the streets, would beat the Judas, and each other too, using an inflated pig's bladder which had been donated by local butchers and tied to the end of a long stick. This wild, noisy but good-humoured rivalry would then culminate on Good Friday in the burning of all the Judases on bonfires on local waste ground.

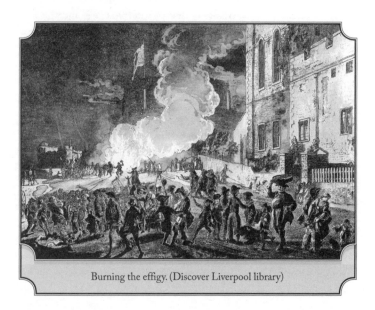

Burning the effigy. (Discover Liverpool library)

This peculiar ceremony appears to be entirely unknown in any other part of Britain, and was also unknown in the rest of Liverpool. It was so localised that even people living in the nearby neighbourhoods in Toxteth and the Dingle never knew about it! It is unclear how this annual celebration originated, although it does take place at Easter time in Greece, Spain and Mexico. Did it come to the Dingle from these countries? Under whatever circumstances this curious custom did arrive in Liverpool's Holy Land, it became a strong tradition there, especially throughout the 1920s and '30s. But after the Second World War it began to die out and had ceased altogether by the late 1950s.

THE EARL AND THE PLAYHOUSE

Ferdinando Stanley (1559–94), Lord Strange and the 5th Earl of Derby, had a passion for the theatre and for performing. So much so that he had his own troupe of actors, known as 'Lord Strange's Players'. The earl and his company not only performed for his family and friends at his home at Knowsley Hall, near the small market town of Prescot, but he also toured with them.

It is believed that William Shakespeare (1564–1616) may also have written for and perhaps performed with Ferdinando. When the 5th Earl died prematurely he was succeeded by his brother, William Stanley (c. 1561–1642). Earl William was determined to enjoy life and to indulge more fully his own passions for music and the theatre, which he had enthusiastically shared with his brother. In fact, he also had his own troupe of players, perhaps 'inherited' from Ferdinando.

Indeed, William Stanley approved, encouraged, and may even have paid for the building of a playhouse in Prescot. It is likely that Lord Derby ordered its construction, not simply to indulge his private passions for the theatre but, also like his brother, to provide entertainment for guests staying with him at Knowsley Hall. This 'theatrum' or 'lusorio', as it is described in the records, was erected after William succeeded to the title and estates, probably around 1595, but certainly before 1599. It was designed and built by Richard, the younger brother of Percival Harrington, who was Lord Derby's steward and who also presided over Prescot's local court.

The town was an important commercial hub in the region, and on market days vast crowds were drawn to Prescot, not only from nearby Liverpool, but from many other towns and villages. The theatre would have been an undoubted added attraction, thus increasing the profits to be made in the small but important town. Named simply as the Playhouse, it was located in Eccleston Street on land technically classed as 'waste', and was constructed in a cockpit design – that is, rows of tiered seating in a horseshoe shape, possibly on two levels. These looked down over a central open space and faced a stage area at the open end of the horseshoe. The whole theatre was enclosed and had a pitched roof over the seating areas. However, the central space was open to the sky and the elements. Audience members who could not afford seats would fill this ground-level area, standing throughout the performance.

It appears that the Playhouse was quite large and, even if not as spectacular as either the Globe or the Rose Theatres in London, it was the first and one of only very few freestanding theatres outside the capital. The Playhouse was also built before the Globe, which was not erected until 1599. It is known that Shakespeare worked at the Globe as well as the Rose (built in 1587), and that he wrote many of his greatest plays for the companies in both theatres.

What is also likely is that he also wrote for and probably performed at the Prescot Playhouse. If so, it is likely that Shakespeare also did so at Knowsley Hall, for both the 5th and 6th Earls of Derby. However, for the past 250 years many people, including noted academics, scholars and – more recently – film producers, have either proposed or supported the idea that some, if not all, of Shakespeare's plays were actually written by someone other than Shakespeare himself. Some of the most frequently cited alter egos are the playwright and poet, Christopher Marlowe (1564–93); the statesman, philosopher and author, Sir Francis Bacon (1561–1626); and even Queen Elizabeth I! Most recently, Edward de Vere, the 17th Earl of Oxford (1550–1604), has been suggested. He was the father-in-law of Earl William Stanley, who is actually himself a candidate for the 'true' identity of Shakespeare.

There are a number of reasons why some people regard this as being perfectly feasible, including the fact that Shakespeare was only

The Globe Theatre in London. The Prescot Theatre would have looked very similar. (Discover Liverpool library)

basically educated, at the local grammar school in Stratford-upon-Avon. He never went to university, nor is there any evidence that he ever travelled abroad. Neither is there evidence of any previous training or writing experience, or access to a library. His parents were illiterate, and so were his wife and children.

Despite this, his plays display considerable knowledge of classical and more contemporary history, the law, literature, social mores of the times and a particular knowledge of how royal courts functioned, especially in northern Italy. However, Lord Derby, as a leading courtier and well-travelled aristocrat, would certainly have had all of this knowledge and considerable personal experience. In fact, he was one of the young nobles who undertook the Grand Tour of Europe specifically to acquire such understanding and skill.

Also, there are gaps in the records of both Earl William and William Shakespeare's lives, and many of these gaps cross-coincide. Some historians and commentators also speculate that perhaps the name 'Shakespeare' was a pseudonym (with typically bawdy Tudor sexual innuendo) and that William Stanley adopted the name as a 'secret dual identity'. This would perhaps enable the stage-struck earl, who was renowned for his wit and provocative sense of humour, to escape his official responsibilities and duties from time to time.

So, was the 'Bard of Avon' actually the 'Bard of Knowsley'? Leaving aside the obvious 'clue' that the playwright and the earl shared the same initials, and that they were roughly the same age, if one combines all this circumstantial evidence it is possible to see how William Stanley might have been the actual author of the plays attributed to William Shakespeare; but the evidence is far from conclusive.

Without any truly credible proof to the contrary, one must conclude that the plays of William Shakespeare were written by William Shakespeare. Whether or not the 6th Earl of Derby did write all or some of these plays is, like the other occasional mysteries associated with the Stanley family (and Shakespeare), something we are unlikely ever to discover.

Fortunately though, the story of the earl and the Playhouse does not end here. The current, and 19th Earl of Derby, is president of Shakespeare North, a charitable trust that is directing the rebuilding of the Prescot Playhouse, which was pulled down early in the seventeenth century. In the spring of 2016, planning permission was granted to build a replica theatre as part of a larger educational and cultural complex, and £27 million was pledged by local and national government to fund the project.

Using theatre designs by Inigo Jones that date from 1629, this will be the only replica of an indoor Jacobean Court theatre in the world. It will seat 460 people and will be home to the world's finest professional touring company, performing Shakespeare's plays. The new Playhouse Theatre and educational complex will be built a few metres away from the original site of the Tudor playhouse, and a 140-seat, multi-use space will also be created alongside studios, education facilities and a café and bar. There will be an education hub, home to a master's degree and diploma in Shakespearean performance and practice.

This will be a fitting memorial and tribute to Shakespeare (whoever else he may or may not have been), and to Earls Ferdinando and William Stanley.

THE PALACE AND THE 'CREEP INN'

The north Wirral seaside resort of New Brighton stands on the Wallasey coast of the River Mersey, directly opposite Crosby, Bootle and north Liverpool. The town was created as a business venture by an imaginative, wealthy Liverpool merchant in the 1830s. His name was James Atherton (1770–1838), and his idea was to build a northern equivalent to the thriving spa town and seaside resort of Brighton on the Sussex coast; hence the name he gave to his new community.

All kinds of tourist amenities and attractions began to appear on the New Brighton beachfront including, in 1871, the Palace Amusement

The Palace amusement complex in the nineteenth century. (Discover Liverpool library)

Arcade. This included a concert room, skating rink, dancing saloon, aquarium, greenhouses and a large theatre. Operettas and musical plays were performed there including a season of Gilbert and Sullivan presented by the D'Oyly Carte Company. In the winter of 1880, a capacious salt water bathing pool was added, which was at the time the largest plunge pool in the country. The Palace certainly drew in the crowds and during the 1882 summer season it averaged 10,000 visitors per week.

The Palace thrived until, in 1916, a disastrous fire almost totally destroyed the building. Fortunately, though, the skating rink and theatre were saved. The entertainment complex was quickly rebuilt by its new owners, the Wilkie family. They completely redesigned and modernised it and it reopened as the New Palace. Now it included a collection of the most modern amusement machines and rides, advertised as an 'all weather palace of fun'.

Always determined to keep pace with the times, the Wilkies completely redesigned and rebuilt the New Palace once again. This was at the massive cost of £11,000! It was then reopened, in 1939, just as the Second World War broke out. All places of public entertainment were immediately closed down by the British Government, including the New Palace, but the building had a secret that suddenly made it very desirable to the War Office: a series of large caves and tunnels that ran, and still do, directly beneath the building.

Almost from the outbreak of the war, this whole subterranean area was made the home of a large munitions workshop. Kept secret from the general public, it was below the New Brighton promenade that over 200 women worked in shifts, night and day, twenty-four hours a day and seven days a week. Their weekly output was 250,000 machine gun bullets, 25,000 shells and 1,400 press-button switches for aircraft radios, essential for the war effort.

In 1941, the Japanese bombed the American naval base at Pearl Harbour in Hawaii, and brought the USA into the war. Within a few weeks of this the main New Palace building was commandeered by the American Army, who used it as a storage depot for the duration of the conflict. In 1942, the Palace Staff Social Club was opened for the munitions and depot workers in one of the caves off the munitions factory. This was named the 'Creep Inn', because you had to be careful not

The Second World War munitions workers beneath the New Palace amusement arcade. (Discover Liverpool library)

to bang your head on the rocks as you went inside. With a bar, dartboard, and plenty of tables and chairs, this proved popular with everyone.

After the war the New Palace was reopened and filled with all the very latest amusement equipment and fairground rides. Once again the public could enjoy all-weather fun, on the 'Gallopers' or 'Bobby Horses', the 'Waltzer', the 'Dodgems' and the 'Jets', amongst many other attractions.

Meanwhile, the munitions machinery was removed and the old factory caves and the Creep Inn were left intact, but unused, although during the 1960s and '70s the former staff social club was reopened as a nightclub. Still owned by the Wilkie family, and currently managed by David Wilkie, the popular entertainment and amusement venue has been renamed as the New Palace and Adventureland. It continues to maintain its place as one of the main attractions on the redeveloping and re-energised New Brighton promenade. There are also speculations that some of the tunnels and caves, and the old Creep Inn, might reopen. Now, that would be something really special …

ABDULLAH QUILLIAM AND BRITAIN'S FIRST MOSQUE

Just further along West Derby Road from where Hengler's Circus and the later Hippodrome once stood is a short row of mid-Victorian houses named Brougham Terrace. For most of the twentieth century, much of this row of properties served as the principal location for the Liverpool City Registrars of Births, Marriages and Deaths.

However, the terrace has a different significance for many residents of the city, in that it was also the location for Britain's first mosque. In fact, the history of the now thriving Muslim community in Britain has quite an unorthodox beginning, being founded as it was by a Liverpudlian!

William Henry Quilliam was born on 10 April 1856, at 22 Elliot Street in the centre of Liverpool. He was the son of a Manx watch-maker and a descendant of Captain John Quilliam RN, who was first lieutenant aboard HMS *Victory*, serving under Admiral Horatio Nelson. Known as Henry by his family, Quilliam was educated at Liverpool Institute School for Boys (now Liverpool Institute for Per-forming Arts – the 'Fame' school). After leaving school he trained and qualified as a solicitor.

Fervently anti-alcohol, Henry was a dedicated socialist and a trade unionist who dedicated himself to supporting the working classes of Liverpool. In 1882, he went to Morocco to recover from an illness brought on by overwork. Here, he developed an interest in the Islamic faith and culture and, in 1887, at the age of 31, he proclaimed himself a Muslim convert. He took the name of Abdullah and after returning to Liverpool he gave a lecture on Islam at the Temperance League Hall in Mount Vernon Street. He began to hold regular meetings there, and soon he had his first convert in Mrs Elisabeth Cates, who took the Islamic name of Fatima.

It was then that the Liverpool Muslim Institute was founded by Quilliam, Cates and their supporters. In 1889, the expanding group moved to their own premises at No. 8 Brougham Terrace, where they established a small mosque in the building – the first mosque in Britain. The money to achieve this came from a donation of 2,300 guineas given to Abdullah by the Amir (ruler) of Afghanistan.

In 1893, this fledgling British Muslim community began to publish a weekly newspaper, *The Crescent*, and later the monthly journal, *The Islamic World*. This latter publication was distributed to more than twenty countries around the world, and was produced using their own printing press, which was operated from the basement in Brougham Terrace.

By the turn of the twentieth century the Liverpool Muslim Institute had 150 members from all walks of life – men, women and children. Soon, they purchased the rest of Brougham Terrace and established a boarding school for boys, a day school for girls, a library, a reading room, a museum and a scientific laboratory. Classes were held in the evenings in a variety of subjects and these were available to all, whether Muslim or not.

The achievements of Abdullah soon spread throughout the Muslim world and, on a visit to Liverpool in 1895, the Sultan of Turkey, who was a leading Muslim, conferred on Quilliam the title of 'Sheikh-ul-Islam of the British Isles'. This title was subsequently confirmed by the Amir of Afghanistan. Now, Muslims of all classes, but especially

Britain's first mosque inside No. 8 Brougham Terrace. (Courtesy of the Abdullah Quilliam Heritage Centre)

seamen from all over the world, came to the Brougham Terrace mosque to pray and to meet Abdullah Quilliam, who was now well known and respected throughout the Muslim world.

Abdullah continued to help people with legal and personal matters. If they were sick he saw to their care. If they died he guaranteed them a Muslim funeral. He even bought land in Liverpool's cemeteries especially for this purpose. He also undertook to contact their relatives and to pass on any property or effects belonging to the deceased.

Abdullah Quilliam.
(Courtesy of the Abdullah
Quilliam Heritage Centre)

By 1907, Islam had begun to spread so widely across Britain that the Liverpool Muslim Institute became the British Muslim Institute and, in 1908, Sheikh Abdullah Quilliam left England on an extended visit to Turkey. Quilliam was such a dynamic personality that soon after his departure the institute went into a decline. The buildings at Brougham Terrace were vacated and the group dispersed. For reasons that have never been discovered, Abdullah never returned to Liverpool, and died in 1932, in London.

He was buried in Brookwood Cemetery near Woking. It was to this town that many of the members of the original Liverpool group had moved, and it was also in Woking that a new Muslim community and mosque were established. Quilliam is buried alongside other prominent British Muslims, including Abdullah Yusuf Ali (1872–1953) and Muhammad Marmaduke Pickthall (1875–1936), who each separately translated the Koran from Arabic into English – for the first time by Pickthall, in 1930, and then by Ali, in 1934.

In 1998, a small group of Liverpool Muslims formed the Abdullah Quilliam Society. Their first significant act was to place a plaque on the front wall of No. 8 Brougham Terrace commemorating the life and works of Sheikh Abdullah. An additional plaque was unveiled outside the prayer room, which had survived in the building, by Mrs Patricia Gordon, Quilliam's granddaughter. The history of the terrace was the subject of a BBC documentary in 2004, when, for the first time and after a lapse of 100 years, formal prayers (salat) were said in the original mosque. These were led by the late Dr M. Akbar Ali (1925–2016), the renowned Indian poet and professor, and at the time the chairman of the Abdullah Quilliam Society.

The present owners of the properties at Brougham Terrace are Liverpool City Council, who operated the Register Office from the premises. The council moved out some years ago and, recognising the historical and cultural importance of the buildings, they offered Brougham Terrace to the Abdullah Quilliam Society at a peppercorn rent. This enabled the society to establish the Abdullah Quilliam Heritage Centre. Thus, No. 8 Brougham Terrace has once again come into the care and management of the local Muslim community.

The Abdullah Quilliam Society has now successfully and beautifully restored the original mosque in the building, together with a number of other rooms. These play a full part in the lives of the Muslim community of Liverpool and beyond. The heritage centre is now part of the wider, non-Muslim community too, taking an active role in the cultural growth and spiritual evolution of the city.

The society also established educational, research and community facilities to promote greater understanding of the Muslim faith, and of its relationship with other religions and traditions. They also provide a place for exhibitions, lectures and seminars; courses in the Arabic language; study workshops; Islamic classes for children and converts and counselling services. The Muslim community right across Merseyside is now a large and thriving one, and numbers approximately 30,000 people.

Most Merseyside Muslims now regularly worship at the Al-Rahma Mosque in Hatherley Street, in Toxteth, and at the smaller mosques near Penny Lane in Liverpool, and in Birkenhead on the Wirral. However, Brougham Terrace has taken its place as a centre of excellence in the many diverse faith communities of Liverpool, and the reopened original British mosque is providing interested visitors with an opportunity to gain a closer understanding of and friendship with the Muslim faith and people.

THE WALLASEY HERMIT

Gotthold Johann Frederick Krüger, known locally and simply as Frederick, or 'the Hermit', came to Liscard in Wallasey around 1878, where he made his home on the sands of the shore in a series of self-built shacks and shanties. He lived in seclusion and obscurity, talking to no one and keeping himself very much to himself.

After ten years he finally settled in a corrugated iron hut off Green Lane in Wallasey, where he continued his solitary reclusive existence for a further twenty years. He was recognisable by his drooping moustache and shabby clothes, and was well known in the district, even though he remained mostly shy and uncommunicative.

By 1905, Frederick had become such a familiar, curious and mysterious character that the local newspaper sent a journalist to interview him. He found that the hermit's metal hut was stacked with sheaves of musical scores by Wagner and Mozart. He was surprised to discover that some manuscripts were compositions by Krüger himself. There were also great piles of books on classical subjects, most written in Latin and Greek. The reporter described the hut as being 15ft long, 6ft wide, 12ft high and partitioned into three separate makeshift rooms. He also said that the entire place was so cluttered that it was hard to move around. This middle-aged hoarder lived entirely alone, except for five retriever dogs that he was devoted to, and which he regularly took for walks along the Wallasey shore.

There was only one person with whom Frederick came into regular contact, a market gardener from Green Lane in Wallasey by the name of Samuel Howard. He took mail in for the hermit, including his small but regular allowance, although he could never find out who was sending this, or why. Frederick called in to see Samuel two or three times a week, to collect any mail and for pails of fresh water, but never for conversation! All he ever said was that he had no friends and just wanted to exist alone and have the right to live his life in study and thought. So Frederick was always a 'man of mystery'.

Early in March 1909, a Wallasey labourer named Charles Webster was working in a field near Krüger's hut. After realising that he had not seen the famous hermit for some time, at 8 a.m. he knocked on the outside of the makeshift home. Getting no reply he peered through a dirty and somewhat obscured window. He thought he saw a body inside so immediately went to the local police station. He returned with a constable who broke into the jumbled and dishevelled shanty. Inside they found the body of the old hermit, dead and kneeling on the floor, with his dogs in a protective group around him. The condition of his body showed that he had been dead for some days. It was only at the resulting inquest, which took place in a packed courtroom, that the facts about Frederick Krüger's past life emerged.

It seemed that he had been born in Prussia, in 1848, where his family had been in the service of the king. Young Frederick had been quite academically gifted and had gone on to graduate from Rostock, Munich and Leipzig Universities. He was a scholar of ancient Greek and Latin, and was fluent in English, French and Italian. He had also been a highly talented and respected concert pianist and composer, but opened a law practice in Berlin.

Frederick then entered the German Diplomatic Corps, shortly after Prussia merged with the other German states to form the German Empire, and was given a posting to Peking. However, for unknown reasons he had not taken up his post and simply left Germany for Britain and Wallasey. He apparently had no relatives in England, and his only real source of income was the small, regular allowance he received from Germany. This was simply not enough for him to live on, so local people who had become quite fond of their local eccentric made sure he never starved and that he was always warm.

Following his death, there being no money to pay for his funeral, again the local people showed their compassion and affection for the old man. The villagers of Liscard and Wallasey clubbed together to give Frederick the best possible funeral they could afford, and paid for a burial plot so he would not lie in a pauper's grave. This meant that his funeral, on 13 March 1909, was a grand affair with the body laid in a magnificent coffin. This was carried in a glass-sided hearse drawn by four black-plumed horses and followed by a number of mourners.

Why this highly educated and clearly talented man gave up his home, profession and social status – as well as a very lucrative income

The funeral of Frederick Krüger – the Wallasey Hermit. (Discover Liverpool library)

– to live out his life in obscure poverty, in a hut on a beach in a Wirral village, was a secret that Frederick took with him to his grave. His burial place, with a headstone also paid for by Wallasey people, is in Rake Lane Cemetery in Liscard; the final resting place of the 'Wallasey Hermit'.

SALTY DUNGEON POINT

Between the southernmost district of Liverpool at Speke, and its nearby neighbour, the tiny, delightful and surprisingly rural township of Hale, a narrow largely unmade road winds down to the River Mersey. This almost entirely uninhabited stretch of coast is known as Dungeon Point and the roadway is known as Dungeon Lane. But this has nothing to do with prisons or incarceration of any form. In fact, it is probably derived from the Anglo-Saxon words 'dunge' or 'denge', meaning 'marshland' or 'land that adjoins marsh'.

Today there is only an isolated farmhouse and some outbuildings standing at Dungeon, surrounded by a large expanse of heathland and sandflats, but at one point this was an important and thriving centre of the salt-refining and shipping trade. Until the ready availability of simple and economic mechanical refrigeration, the usual way to preserve food was to either cure it, or liberally coat or pack it in salt. For meat and fish in particular this slowed the decaying process, or at least disguised the taste of its rottenness! This was especially important in a seafaring town like Liverpool, where long sea voyages needed great quantities of long-lasting provisions, and where salted meat was in great demand.

The local salt-refining trade really developed following the discovery of rock salt near Runcorn in Cheshire, in 1670. In 1697, a salt refinery with a processing centre and a sandstone quay was established at Dungeon by Sir Thomas Johnson (1644–1728). He served as both MP and Mayor of Liverpool and Sir Thomas Street was named after him.

It was to Dungeon that flatboats and barges brought rock salt from the Cheshire salt fields at Northwich, Middlewich, Nantwich and Winsford. It was then refined and shipped onwards. The refining process involved the dissolving of rock salt in seawater from the

Mersey, which was heated in large metal pans over coal fires. The volume of salt produced using this basic method was considerable, as were the quantities of coal needed to continuously operate the burners. This kept the salt, coalmining and transportation trades in the area both active and profitable for their owners.

Salt then became a major export from the port of Liverpool because, as well as preserving food on Liverpool vessels, it was an essential commodity for the Newfoundland cod fisheries. From there salted fish was shipped all around the world, but especially to the West Indies where it was used to feed slaves on the plantations. It was also prized because it could be profitably traded for expensive commodities, such as coffee and sugar. Salt was particularly essential, though, in iron and steel foundries and in the pottery industry. It was also used in certain chemical processes, which is why the chemical industry grew up so rapidly in Cheshire, close to the salt fields.

In 1746, the Dungeon refinery was acquired by John Ashton (d. 1759). He was another merchant who soon become wealthy and significant in the life of Liverpool. He also went into the slave trade, the profits from which he successfully invested in the building of the Sankey Canal. This opened in 1757, as one of England's first true industrial waterways. Also profiting from the Liverpool salt trade at this time were the Blackburne family, from Orford near Warrington. John Blackburne (1694–1786) had a salt refinery at Garston, close to Dungeon, and he also successfully developed a major salt refinery in Liverpool. This was adjacent to Liverpool's – and the world's – first commercial enclosed wet dock, which opened in 1715. Known as the Old Dock, the site of this is now in the heart of the modern city's retail centre, Liverpool ONE. John went on to become Lord Mayor of Liverpool in 1760.

Blackburne's Liverpool salt refinery became so important that the town's second dock, South Dock, which opened in 1753, soon became known by the name it retains today, Salthouse Dock. This was because of the salt warehouses erected there to service Blackburne's refinery and vessels, which then sailed from that dock. Blackburne traded with Johnson and Ashton and they all became extremely rich and powerful. In 1788 John's grandson, Jonathan Blackburne (1754–1833), began building a grand mansion for his family, named Blackburne House,

Liverpool's Salthouse Dock in the nineteenth century.
(Liverpool Athenaeum library)

which still stands on what is now Hope Street in the city. In common with many Liverpool businessmen at this time, the Blackburnes also profited from the slave trade. Jonathan in particular fought vociferously for its retention as the abolitionist movement began to become increasingly vocal in the town.

From the mid-eighteenth century and through the nineteenth century, the estuary of the Mersey was increasingly used for transporting salt and coal, as well as many other commodities. Even so, by the late 1840s, and for reasons that are unclear, the salt works closed at Dungeon and its wharves and quays were then taken over by a firm of ship-breakers. It was here that schooners, paddle steamers and, on one occasion, a Victorian warship were taken apart. However, as the river channels near Speke and Hale began to silt up, the shipyard closed, in 1912.

All industry then ceased at Dungeon and it reverted once more to being an ignored backwater, with only a few isolated homes and post-industrial riverfront. All that can now be seen at Dungeon Point are a small part of the sandstone quay and some rubble and broken rocks. This is all that is left behind from the salt refinery that once dominated this now almost desolate stretch of the Mersey foreshore.

THE GREAT LEPRECHAUN HUNT

'The Great Leprechaun Hunt and Flying Saucer Scare' happened simultaneously in two places on Merseyside in the summer of 1964: at Edge Hill in Liverpool and in the town of Kirkby.

On the night of Tuesday, 30 June, a 9-year-old boy, in a state of shock and very excited, told his parents that he had seen something very strange in the park known as Kensington Gardens, near his Jubilee Drive home in Edge Hill. He was reported in the *Daily Post* as saying, 'Last night I saw little men in white hats throwing stones and mud at each other on the bowling green. Honest mister, I did.'

The rumour spread, and not only children but adults too were soon scouring the park, and private gardens in nearby streets, frantically searching for little men. They were tearing up shrubs and plants, and burrowing around bushes, hedges and trees, and by the second night, 1 July, the park, its covered reservoir and its adjacent bowling green was swamped with crowds. The police had to entirely clear the park and guard it from the marauding leprechaun hunters.

But that night the story took a new twist. A woman from Crosby, just to the north of Liverpool, reported that on 1 July she had seen 'Strange objects glistening in the sky whizzing over the River Mersey to the city from the Irish Sea'. On 2 July, this story continued in the press, with more and more people saying that they had seen mysterious creatures, and describing them as 'little green men in white hats throwing stones and tiny clods of earth at one another'.

The park policeman on duty in Kensington Gardens on 1 and 2 July had to wear a crash helmet. This was to protect himself from the children who had taken to throwing stones around the park and into the shrubbery, in their attempts to force the little green men out into the open. The officer told a reporter from the local paper:

> This all started on Tuesday. How I just don't know, but the sooner it ends the better. Stones have been thrown on the bowling green and for the second night running no one has been able to play. The kids just won't go away. Some swear they have seen leprechauns. The story has gone round and now we are being besieged with leprechaun hunters.

The violence of the stone-throwing got so bad that the police had to set up a temporary first-aid shelter to treat at least a dozen children who suffered cuts and bruises. It was at this point in the story that, suddenly, little green leprechauns were also reported in Kirkby, specifically in and around the grounds of St Chad's Church. Also, a story in the *Kirkby Reporter* appeared about flying saucers being sighted over the town, as well as little green men, with witnesses describing 'a strange object in the sky, which changed the colour of its lights from red to silver, and that moved slowly at first, then very fast'. People now came forward to say that the little green visitors were about 8in high, with red and green tunics, blue knee-britches, green boots and white hats. They also said that they had heard them speaking in a strong Irish brogue.

So, were these strange little green men aliens or actually Irish leprechauns? Had they flown to Kirby from the Emerald Isle in glowing, multi-coloured flying machines?

By this time, what had begun as a small band of curious children around St Chad's had grown to a vast crowd of about 200. They had invaded the graveyard, hunting in and around the tombs including those of the former Earls of Sefton, and were causing general pandemonium. It took a lot of persuasion from the vicar to convince them they were wasting their time.

But the determined crowds of hunting children simply shifted to new territories, particularly St Marie's RC Primary School, and St Mary Mother of God Church in Northwood. Here they began again, running amok and burrowing in the shrubs and hedgerows on their hands and knees, desperately searching for the 'Little People'. But the tiny men remained elusive and none were ever found, either in Kensington or in Kirkby; and no pots of gold either!

For many years no one could be sure if the great leprechaun hunts were simply the results of mass hysteria, or something else; especially as so many people, adults as well as children, were prepared to come forward as eyewitnesses. Then, on 26 January 1982, a possible explanation appeared in an article in the *Liverpool Echo*. In this a man from Kensington by the name of Brian Jones, who was quite a small man, said that back in the summer of 1964 he had been doing some gardening in a house that backed onto Kensington Gardens.

He was in his gardening clothes, which consisted of a white woollen hat with a red bobble on the top, a red waistcoat and a denim shirt, a pair of navy blue trousers and green wellies, and he was smoking a pipe as he worked. He said that he had seen some children sitting on the 10ft high wall that separated the garden from the park. One of them spotted Brian in the tall grass, pointed at him and said to his friends, 'Ey look, it's a leprechaun!'

Realising that his shortness, and the fact that he was standing in the middle of a patch of very high weeds must have made him

One of the 'Little People'.
(Discover Liverpool library)

look like one of the Little People, he decided to play a trick on them. So he started to jump up and down, waving his arms at the now startled children and babbling at them in gibberish. Then he picked up some turves of grass and started to throw them at the children, who now jumped off the wall and ran off across the park in a panic. The following night Brian was in the garden again and wearing the same outfit. He heard quite a commotion coming from the park and, climbing up his stepladder and looking over the top of the wall, he saw around 300 children in the park. Almost immediately some of the children saw him and shouted out, 'There he is! There's the leprechaun!'

But they did not come any closer. So, Brian said, he decided to repeat his antics from the previous night. Off he went again, shouting out gibberish and waving wildly at his large audience from the top of his ladder, and throwing more turves into the air. After about five minutes or so of this he grew bored with his game and went indoors. For the next few nights he and his neighbours were plagued with children climbing over their garden walls and knocking on the front doors of Jubilee Drive, asking for the leprechaun!

As the rumours spread and more and more people invaded the park, Brian decided to keep quiet about his 'leprechaun act', only admitting to it twenty years later in the newspaper article. Probably a wise move really, considering all the trouble he had caused. Despite Brian's confession there are some people who remain convinced that the leprechauns they saw as children were the real thing. Others are just as convinced that they were indeed little green men from a flying saucer!

Whatever you choose to believe is entirely up to you …

A Taste of Scouse

Liverpudlians find fun in food and in sharing it with family and friends. Of course, our local delicacy is scouse, from which is derived the name of our dialect and also the name by which we are best known – Scousers. However, and contrary to popular opinion, our traditional dish is not related to either Irish stew or Lancashire hot pot. It is, in fact, of Scandinavian seafaring origin.

Indeed, eighteenth-century Liverpool sailors would have known the dish well, sailing and trading as they did with Nordic sailors and ships, especially in the whaling boats of the Baltic Fleet that sailed out of Liverpool's Wapping Dock. Seafaring has always been a dangerous occupation; only for the hardiest of souls. The work is hard, often in appalling conditions and the foulest of weathers, and sailors need food that will warm and nourish them, especially in freezing northern waters. This was particularly true in the eighteenth and nineteenth centuries. However, British sailors, including those from Liverpool, would often have had to survive on a diet of rancid salt pork, accompanied by weevil-infested biscuits and washed down with stale water.

When in Scandinavian ports such as Stavanger, Oslo, Copenhagen, Malmo and Stockholm, the sailors from Liverpool and other parts of Britain would exchange news and tall tales with their Nordic counterparts. But, whilst their shared stories would often be about wine, women and song, it is undoubtedly true that 'the way to a man's heart is through his stomach'! They were impressed and envious when told that a regular meal on board Scandinavian vessels was a nourishing and warming stew that they called 'lobscouse'. This name appears to have come from the Norwegian word '*lapskous*', meaning 'spoon meat' or 'stew'.

The first written reference to this food was made by the early eighteenth-century writer, Ned Ward, in his book about ships and seafaring, *The Wooden World Dissected*. Written in 1708, he describes seamen eating 'a baked food of spare meat and vegetables' called 'lobscouse'.

So, English sailors in general, and Liverpool matelots in particular, soon got to know the dish well and adopted it as a staple food aboard their own ships. But they now called it 'scouse', as a shortened form of 'lobscouse'. The meal was ideal to eat at sea because it could be very quickly prepared using cheap or leftover cuts of meat, such as lamb. Plain root vegetables were essential, in particular potatoes, and then perhaps carrots, turnips or onions. These were just as inexpensive and readily available, and were roughly chopped and added to the meat. Covered with water and seasoned with salt (or often with just a pail of seawater), this could then be left to stew slowly on a hob for an indefinite period without needing to be watched.

When meat was unavailable or too expensive the stew would be made as a plain potato and vegetable broth, with perhaps the addition of a grain such as barley or crushed ship's biscuits, as a thickening. This was known as 'blind scouse' – today, we would refer to this as 'the vegetarian option'!

Scouse soon became a very convenient meal for sailors. This was because it could be eaten at any time when their duties at sea permitted, especially following rough weather or in cold and stormy conditions, when something hearty, warming and tasty to eat was a real necessity. Liverpudlian sailors took the recipe with them wherever they sailed around the world, and became known as 'Scousers' as a result. They also brought it back home, and on shore scouse soon became the food of sailors' families and poorer people, for the same reasons. Because of its capacity to cheaply and easily fill empty stomachs the popularity of scouse grew. By the late eighteenth century it was becoming a widely familiar dish and was fully established in Liverpool, and well beyond the port too, by the nineteenth century.

In the early twentieth century, as social conditions improved and stabilised, the recipe became fixed to consist largely of lamb, onions and carrots, with lots of 'old' potatoes that will 'fall' during the cooking process, thus thickening the broth. Scouse became a cheap and easy staple during and between both world wars, and there were particular surges in its popularity in the late 1950s and early '60s. Even in the late 1980s and early '90s, it was a rare Liverpudlian household indeed that did not feature scouse in the family menu, occasionally if not regularly.

At the beginning of the twenty-first century scouse is once again a popular dish that can found on the menu of many cafés, restaurants, pubs and clubs all over the city. However, beef is most commonly used in the dish now, although a truly authentic scouse should be made only with lamb. This really is a matter of taste, of course, as both ingredients make a truly delicious meal, but they do have very different final flavours and appearances.

Scouse is still an important staple in poorer households, but it has now also become a 'stylish' and 'trendy' meal. Pubs serve it more than ever before and many such hostelries offer periodic 'Scouse Nights', which are always popular. If you get the opportunity to try scouse do

A plate of scouse with all the trimmings.
(Discover Liverpool library)

seize this; you will thoroughly enjoy the meal and I am sure it will become one of your own favourites.

Better still, why not cook it yourself? If you follow my own tried and trusted recipe, passed down the female line of my family for six generations (with my own twentieth-century additions), then you cannot fail!

INGREDIENTS

4–6oz diced stewing beef, or shoulder of lamb, for each guest (do
not over trim as the fat helps to flavour and thicken the broth).

I large potato for each guest, cut into six or eight large, even chunks
(potatoes should be 'old' potatoes, such as King Edwards or Maris
Pipers, which will 'fall' during cooking).

½ medium sized carrot for each guest, sliced, but not too thinly.

¼ of a large Spanish onion for each guest, roughly chopped.

Enough stock (appropriate to the meat being cooked) to completely
cover the ingredients in the cooking pot.

Salt and ground black pepper for seasoning.

When making a beef stock (rather than just a bucket of seawater!) I suggest using one or two Oxo cubes, or a tablespoon of Bovril to enhance the flavour. You can also use any other good quality stock cubes you have to hand. For a lamb stock, a couple of lamb or chicken stock cubes are ideal, or again, something of similar quality.

My secret ingredient is a few good dashes of Worcestershire sauce, added into the scouse in the final twenty minutes or so of the cooking. This will really lift the flavour.

If preparing a 'blind scouse' for vegetarian guests simply leave out the meat, of course, and you may wish to add extra vegetables for volume. If so, I suggest either turnip (not swede) or leeks, but do use a good vegetable stock for the broth. Adding a little thyme, some sage and a bay leaf is my own 'special' secret for this version of scouse.

METHOD

1 In a large, heavy frying pan, quickly but lightly brown the meat in
a little oil.

2 Transfer the meat to a large, heavy cooking pot: scouse is stewed
on a hob, not baked or casseroled in an oven.

3 Quickly stir fry the chopped onions, in the same pan used for
frying the meat. Add to the scouse pot.

4 Add the sliced carrots to the scouse pot. Season the mixture well, to taste.

5 Cover the mixture completely with stock.

6 Leaving the pot uncovered, slowly bring the mixture to a boil, stirring occasionally, and then reduce the heat to a simmer. Check the seasoning.

7 Now cover the pot, and continue simmering gently on a very low heat until the potatoes have fallen, stirring occasionally.

8 Check the seasoning again.

9 Keep cooking gently until the meat is tender and the broth has thickened. If it has not thickened enough, and just before the meat begins to fall apart, you can rapidly raise the heat and reduce the stew.

SERVING SUGGESTIONS

You will now have a basic but tasty and nutritious scouse that can be reheated easily if necessary. This makes it a good dish to prepare in advance for a family meal or party. Scouse also freezes and defrosts well, so you can make lots of it and save it for those cold and rainy days. But whichever type of scouse you prepare, how you present and then eat it are critical:

1 Serve great scoops of the broth on large, warm dinner plates, and make plenty of it because everyone will want seconds!

2 Ensure that there is plenty of crusty bread on the side, to dip into the scouse and to wipe your plate clean with afterwards so that nothing is missed or wasted.

3 Pickled red cabbage and sliced beetroot are essential side dishes, and do not be ashamed to garnish your plate of scouse with dollops of thick brown sauce, or a few extra dashes of Worcestershire sauce.

If you are on your own and need cheering up, a good pan of scouse will do it every time. It has that home-cooked, 'mother-used-to-make-it' taste and texture that we all need to give us a lift from time to time.

Planning a dinner or buffet party? Scouse is easy and inexpensive to make, and is a sure-fire winner because it is so unusual at 'posh do's'. Serve it with all the trimmings, though! Your guests and their stomachs will thank you.

AND TO DRINK?

A large mug of steaming, strong Yorkshire tea or a large glass of full-bodied red wine are excellent accompaniments. However, best of all is a huge glass of your favourite British beer, such as Newcastle Brown, Ruddles, Flowers Bitter, Old Speckled Hen, Bombardier, London Pride, Bishops Finger or Beamish Red.

Under no circumstances, though, should you drink lager with your scouse – that is a heresy!

The author preparing one of his celebrated pans of scouse. (Discover Liverpool library)

The darker ales like Guinness and Beamish Black are also good with scouse, although their flavours could be a little intense against the thickness of the broth. But, whatever you drink, make it very good and very large!

All that remains for me to do now is to wish you 'Bon Appétit!' Or, as we can sometimes be heard to say in Liverpool, 'Gerrit down yer lad. It'll stick ter yer ribs on de way down, warm der cockles of yer 'eart, an' purra back on yer like a ware'ouse cat!'

THE BIRD-MAN OF SPEKE

The southernmost 'lost village' of Liverpool is the district of Speke, which borders with the township of Hale. It is famous for its industrial estate, its ancient stately home, Speke Hall, and for what was Britain's first airport outside London, Speke Airport, now renamed as Liverpool John Lennon Airport.

It was at Speke Airport, on 21 May 1956, that the annual Speke Air Show was held, with a crowd of over 120,000 people eagerly expecting to be amazed and thrilled by the aircraft, the displays, and by some spectacular attractions. Not least of these was going to be the attempt by a French parachutist to fly using his own set of 'wings'.

Known by the press and public alike as the 'Bird-Man', Léo Valentin was going to try to achieve something that had already killed around seventy-two men, each of whom had tried and failed to make similar daredevil flights. But Valentin was undaunted and determined to consolidate his reputation as the first man to successfully fly without the aid of any form of motorised propulsion.

Léon Alfred Nicolas Valentin had been born in Epinal, France, in 1919, and had joined the French Armée de L'Air at the age of 19, with the ambition of becoming one of the brand new breed of 'parachutists'. However, he was not able to realise his ambition right away; this had to wait until the Second World War when he escaped from Nazi-occupied France to the relative safety of Morocco.

Wanting to fight the Nazis, he made his way to Liverpool and from there to Glasgow. It was here that, at last, he received training as a paratrooper so that he could be dropped back into his homeland, behind enemy lines. This he did in 1944, and fought bravely and fiercely against the Germans as a saboteur.

Back in France after the war and still in the French Army, Valentin became fascinated by the concept of freefall parachuting (what we now call 'sky-diving'). His object was to jump from a plane flying as high as practical and then to only open his parachute at the last possible moment. This would be at the known minimum height of 9,000ft above ground. Any lower than this would mean that the parachute would not open in time to guarantee a safe landing. In 1947, Valentin made the world's first freefall parachute jump, dropping a distance of 1,800ft from the plane before opening his chute at 9,000ft and landing safely.

Léo Valentin – the Bird-Man of Speke. (Discover Liverpool library)

Next, he wanted to see how high he could drop from, and how far he could freefall before reaching minimum safe distance. In February 1948 he jumped from a plane flying high over Paris and set a record for the longest freefall without a respirator, by dropping 15,600ft before pulling his ripcord. His next freefall drop was for an amazing 20,200ft.

It was at this point that Valentin left the army and was able to take his freefall experiments even further. Now he wanted to see if he could fly as well as freefall. In other words, gain forward controlled movement, instead of simply dropping. This meant that he needed wings as well as a parachute.

His first attempt at a 'wing jump flight' was in 1950 when, wearing a pair of homemade canvas wings, he again leapt from a plane above Paris. In front of a crowd of around 300,000 spectators he began a gliding descent in a broad spiral, but he could not make any forward headway. In fact, at one point he had great difficulty in preventing his flexible wings from wrapping themselves around him, and he went into a rapid vertical spin. Fortunately, he managed to get his canvas wings back into their outstretched position just in time to pull his ripcord at the safe minimum height from the ground. Once again he landed safely, but was extremely shaken. He made one more attempt using canvas wings but with the same unnerving result, so he decided it was time to redesign his apparatus and go for solid wooden wings instead.

During his earlier period as a parachutist, Valentin had been prone to sudden panic attacks as he was making his descents. Now, during the high-speed freefall part of his jumps, he would often freeze before regaining his self-control and pulling the ripcord on his parachute. He also had great difficulty sleeping, frequently suffering dreadful dreams of falling to a brutal and bloody death. These panic attacks and nightmares stayed with him as he now developed his winged flying experiments and displays.

His next pair of wings were made from balsa wood, hinged either side of a central panel that Valentin strapped to his back. But on his first attempt with these, and almost immediately after beginning his freefalling descent, the wind pressure forced his wings to fold backwards. He almost crashed to earth until he used all of his strength to force them back into a spread out position.

For his next attempt, in 1954, Valentin fitted a locking device to keep his wings rigid and, without any crowds of spectators on this occasion, he began his jump. It went very well, and his freefall descent was more stable and his gliding spiral more controlled. After landing, he excitedly claimed that this time he had actually managed to truly fly, and for a distance of 3 miles. However, his panic attacks continued and these also made him extremely superstitious.

Léo Valentin travelled to many countries giving his 'Bird-Man' displays, but he had established a ritual of always loudly shouting out, 'One, two, three!' just before he made a jump from a plane. As well as this he made sure that he only stayed in hotel rooms numbered '123', and no one was ever allowed to touch, handle, move or store his wings, except himself.

One wonders why, if he suffered so badly from these feelings of panic and doom, why the Frenchman wasso obsessed with the desire to fly? Why did he put himself through such stress and anguish? When asked this, he answered:

> When I fly … suddenly I have a sensation of great well-being. Had it not been for the wind I might be motionless in the sky, reclining face downward on the cushions of air through which I am plunging, almost without stirring. It is so different from the normal twisting that for a moment I am scared. It seems impossible that it can be so easy, so agreeable, so intoxicating in its smoothness.
>
> This revelation leaves me at one and the same time numb and yet deeply moved in spirit. There is no reason why one should not fall like this until the end of time, in an element whose sense of lightness no adjective can conjure up. How wonderful it would be to fall asleep in this state of ineffable ease.

But then came the Speke Air Show, and Léo Valentin's attempt to amaze yet another crowd of excited spectators with his remarkable daredevil stunt flying.

On that clear and sunny May afternoon in 1956, the plane took off from the Speke Airport runway and soon began circling high above the upturned and expectant faces of the crowds. Valentin positioned himself at the door of the plane and then, after shouting out his usual 'One, two, three!', he launched himself into space.

However, just as he left the aircraft one of his wings caught against the doorway and he immediately went into a spin. It was clear to the crew on board the plane, and to those on the ground who were watching him through binoculars, that he could not regain control and open his wings. It was also obvious that one of the wings had been badly damaged. Valentin simply plunged towards the ground, gaining speed as he desperately attempted to put his wings into a flying position. But he could not.

Then, a strong gust of wind took hold of the powerless skydiver and carried him away from the airfield. He was seen to pull on the ripcord of his parachute and, to everyone's relief, it opened. But, it did not deploy. Now, as his parachute tangled itself around Valentin's broken wings, screams of horror and cries of helplessness went up from the previously happy crowd watching below. Everyone now realised that the 'Bird-Man' was doomed.

The tragic parachutist fell to earth in a field in nearby Halewood. When his body was recovered, he was found to be lying face down wrapped in a mangled mess of parachute silk, cords and shattered balsa wood. However, there was not a mark on Valentin's body and no blood spilt. Nor were there any appalling injuries and, quite mysteriously, he looked as if he was simply asleep. But the Bird-Man was indeed dead, and the people who first reached him on the ground covered him over with the parachute silk as a final mark of respect to the great daredevil aeronaut.

The body of Léo Valentin was flown back to France, and he was buried with full military honours at the Church of Saint-Sauveur, in Haute-Saône, on 3 June 1956.

ALMOST THE BUNBURY

For generations the Earls of Derby have loved horse racing, and they have bred many champions over the centuries. Edward Smith-Stanley, the 12th Earl of Derby (1752–1834), owned a country house named The Oaks, just outside Epsom, near Leatherhead in Surrey. It was here that he had the idea of creating a new horse race for a different category of animal. This would be run across the Epsom Downs, where popular horse races had been run for some time, but over a shorter distance than the standard 2 miles. In fact, this competition would be run over a flat, straight course that was exactly 1 mile long.

To guarantee the fitness of the animals and so increase the excitement, the race was restricted to 3-year-old fillies, each carrying the same weight. (A filly is a female horse under 4 years old, and its male equivalent is a colt.) The race was run as a 'sweepstake', which is a race in which the owner of each entered horse has to pay an equal amount of money, or 'stake', into the race fund. This is then awarded to the owner of the winning animal. The term is also applied when any group, or 'syndicate' of people, racehorse owners or otherwise, stake money on a race. The name derives from the fact that the winner is the person who 'sweeps' or takes all the stakes in a race. The principal still forms the core of modern racing and, if an owner's horse runs but falls, the stake money is forfeit. However, if the horse is withdrawn before the start of the race then a penalty only is payable.

Named after his house, Lord Derby inaugurated the Oaks Stakes, which was first run on 14 May 1779. To his great satisfaction this race was won by his own horse, 'Bridget'. Instantly, the Oaks proved to be very popular, becoming the annual 'Classic' racing event that still thrives today.

Following the success of the Oaks, Lord Derby, at a dinner with his friend, Sir Charles Bunbury, 6th Baronet (1740–1821), was discussing the need for another new race. This would be run over the same course as the Oaks, but would be open to 3-year-old colts as well as 3-year-old fillies. Once they had agreed the criteria for the race Derby and Bunbury had to decide on a name for it. Each gentleman wanted it to be named after himself so, to settle the matter in true sporting tradition, they decided to toss a coin, which Lord Derby won. This is just as well really, or what we now know as the Derby might well have been called 'the Bunbury'!

The inaugural race was held on 4 May 1780. Fortunately for Sir Charles, even though he had lost the coin toss, his horse 'Diomed' resoundingly beat the rest of the field, winning his owner the considerable sum of £1,065 15s in prize money.

The official name for the race soon became the Epsom Derby Stakes, and the first Wednesday in June became the annual date when the race

Edward Smith-Stanley, the 12th Earl of Derby.
(Discover Liverpool library)

was run, now also becoming known as the 'Blue Ribbon of the Turf'. However, from 1995, 'Derby Day' became either the first or second Saturday in June.

The Oaks, because it was just for fillies, also became known as 'the Ladies' Race', and is held at Epsom on the day before the Derby. This championship competition soon became the most popular horse race in the annual flat-racing season (this runs from the end of March until November), and winning it is regarded as being a peak in the career of both owner and rider.

As with other sporting fixtures around the world, the name 'Derby' is now applied to a number of horse races on the flat, but there is still only one, official 'Derby' classic horse race.

Thank heavens Bunbury lost that coin toss!

REVENGE IN THE COMMONS

Arguably, Britain's most unremarkable prime minister was Spencer Perceval MP (1762–1812); he is notable simply because he was the only British premier to have been assassinated. His murderer was John Bellingham (*c.* 1771–1812), a shipping merchant and insurance broker from Duke Street in Liverpool, who was married with two children.

In 1804, whilst on a business trip to the Arctic Russian port of Archangel, Bellingham was accused of being in debt for the sum of 2,000 roubles, which the broker denied and refused to pay. He was arrested, and although still vehemently denying his guilt, he was sentenced to five years in prison. It was small consolation to Bellingham that he was treated reasonably well and allowed to move freely about the prison, but he knew he should not be there. He had appealed directly to the English Consul for assistance and also to the British ambassador at St Petersburg. They both refused to get involved. Serving his full sentence, Bellingham was eventually released in 1809, and he returned to Liverpool.

He immediately tried to get compensation from the British Government for his mistreatment. He firmly believed that, because their representatives had failed to come to his aid, they were ultimately responsible for his long and unjustified incarceration. However, once again officialdom would not entertain his case. For the next three years Bellingham persisted, petitioning first the Privy Council and then the Treasury, just as fruitlessly.

He next requested that his local MP for Liverpool, General Isaac Gascoigne (*c.* 1763–1841), formally petition Parliament on his behalf. Bellingham wrote to his MP a number of times, but Gascoigne, also known as 'Cunning Isaac' and generally recognised as incompetent and entirely self-serving, refused absolutely. He declared that his constituent's case had no merit and most certainly did not deserve his attention. He was far too busy vigorously campaigning to retain the slave trade, fighting against the abolition of bull-baiting, and opposing the emancipation of Roman Catholics!

Bellingham also wrote to the Prince Regent, later King George IV (1762–1830), and received yet another rejection. When this appeal was also denied, Bellingham then wrote directly to the prime minister himself, Spencer Perceval. When Perceval also refused to become involved the Liverpool businessman became increasingly frustrated and bitter. So, on 23 March 1812, Bellingham's final and quite unusual course of action was to write to the police magistrates in London:

SIRS,

I much regret its being my lot to have to apply to your worships under most peculiar and novel circumstances. For the particulars of the case I refer to the enclosed letter of Mr Secretary Ryder, the notification from Mr Perceval, and my petition to Parliament, together with the printed papers herewith.

The affair requires no further remark than that I consider his Majesty's Government to have completely endeavoured to close the door of justice, in declining to have, or even to permit, my grievances to be brought before Parliament for redress, which privilege is the birthright of every individual.

The purport of the present is, therefore, once more to solicit his Majesty's Ministers, through your medium, to let what is right and proper be done in my instance, which is all I require.

Should this reasonable request be finally denied, I shall then feel justified in executing justice myself – in which case I shall be ready to argue the merits of so reluctant a measure with his Majesty's Attorney-General, wherever and whenever I may be called upon so to do.

In the hopes of averting so abhorrent but compulsive an alternative I have the honour to be, sirs, your very humble and obedient servant,

JOHN BELLINGHAM.

This implied threat of physical violence against an unnamed target was passed to the British Treasury. In response, a Mr Hill asked Bellingham to come and see him. Expecting, at last, to be taken seriously, Bellingham was appalled when Hill informed him that he still had no legitimate grievance, and insisted that he stop his hectoring of the government, its departments, and its ministers.

Bellingham was outraged and a Court report at the time states:

This [Bellingham] declared he considered a carte blanche to take justice into his own hands, and he accordingly determined to take such measures of revenge as he madly supposed would effectually secure that attention and consideration for his case which he deemed it had not received, and to which it was in his opinion fully entitled.

This was when John Bellingham decided to 'punish' the prime minister; the person he felt bore the ultimate responsibility for his suffering.

Monday, 11 May 1812 was a sunny day. It was early evening when Prime Minister Perceval entered the House of Commons and made his way through the lobby towards the chamber. Bellingham had been sitting quietly and unobtrusively in a corner of the lobby, making no attempt to either conceal or draw attention to himself. As the prime minister began to walk past him the disgruntled Liverpudlian stood up and took a pistol from a special pocket he had made inside his overcoat. Bellingham then pointed the weapon at the unsuspecting politician and fired a single shot at point blank range.

The pistol ball struck Perceval in the chest and he immediately cried out, 'I am murdered!' He then staggered and fell to the floor. Still alive but mortally wounded, Perceval was carried to the Speaker's apartments by a number of men. Meanwhile, his attacker simply walked back to

John Bellingham shoots the prime minister in the lobby of the House of Commons. (Liverpool Athenaeum library)

his corner and sat down again. A doctor was summoned whilst the ashen prime minister was placed on a table. He said nothing more, but uttered one or two pain-racked sobs. However, some reports have the dying man clambering up off the table, reeling a short distance, and then crying out, 'I'll have one of Belamey's veal pies!', before collapsing in delirium. By the time the doctor arrived Spencer Perceval was dead. He was 49 years old and left a devoted wife and twelve children.

Meanwhile, back in the lobby, someone shouted, 'Shut the door! Let no one out!', and then someone else called, 'Where's the murderer?'

Bellingham, who was still holding the pistol, answered, 'I am the unfortunate man!'

He was immediately seized, ironically by General Gascoigne, the very Liverpool MP who had failed to help him and who immediately took possession of the pistol. Bellingham said nothing else, but reports describe him as sweating heavily and finding great difficulty in breathing. When searched, Bellingham was found to have another primed and loaded pistol inside his coat, so this was also carefully removed. The Speaker of the House now ordered that Bellingham be taken to the sergeant at arms' quarters for questioning. Throughout, the assassin remained calm and collected and offered no resistance. In fact, he immediately admitted to the murder and said, 'I have been denied the redress of my grievances by government. I have been ill-treated. They all know who I am and what I am. I am a most unfortunate man and feel here sufficient justification for what I have done.'

By this time, news of the prime minister's shooting had reached beyond the walls of the Parliament building. The authorities now feared that there might be outbreaks of violent support for the killer and possible attempts at his rescue. This was a time when revolution was rife across the continent of Europe so these fears were not unfounded; the government of the day was deeply unpopular, and the gap between ordinary people and the rich and powerful was very wide indeed.

When a coach arrived at around 8 p.m. to take Bellingham to prison, a mob had indeed gathered outside. Some of them surged towards the prisoner in an attempt to help him escape, and they had to be forced back. Bellingham was taken back inside the Parliament building again until a contingent of troops arrived at around midnight. Soon after 1 a.m., and with much of the angry mob now dispersed, these armed soldiers now escorted the coach with Bellingham aboard to Newgate Gaol. Here, he was chained and secured in a cell, but he simply lay down and almost immediately fell asleep.

On the advice of his defence council, John Bellingham pleaded 'not guilty' to the charge of murder, but he was certainly resigned to his fate, which was inevitable. The tragic Liverpool businessman was tried in an overcrowded courtroom at the Old Bailey on Friday, 15 May. The trial report states:

> At length Bellingham appeared, and advanced to the bar with a firm step, and quite undismayed. He bowed to the Court most respectfully, and even gracefully; and it is impossible to describe the impression which his appearance, accompanied by this unexpected fortitude, produced. He was dressed in a light brown surtout coat and striped yellow waistcoat; his hair plainly dressed, and without powder.

During the hearing, which lasted for only a day, a journalist reported that he remembered previously seeing Bellingham on a number of occasions in the visitors' gallery of the House of Commons. He had been noted repeatedly asking people to point out significant MPs and Cabinet members to him, including the prime minister. As far as the Court was concerned this showed that he had planned his attack and so proved intent. This also meant that when his lawyer mounted a plea of insanity this was ruled out by the Court.

In his testimony, Bellingham firmly declared that he had no personal animosity towards Perceval, and he seemed to show genuine remorse for the prime minister's death and for the fate of the politician's family. He declared that the only motive for the shooting had been 'want of redress and denial of justice'.

Inevitably, Bellingham was found guilty and sentenced to be hanged, and that his body be 'dissected and anatomised'. However, on the eve of his execution, John Bellingham received a message that two gentlemen from Liverpool had called at Newgate, with assurances that he was to have no concern because they would ensure that his wife and children would be well taken care of and would want for nothing.

Sympathy for his case, and for his attempts to thwart government, was widespread in Liverpool and a subscription had already been taken up in the town to raise a fund for his family. When Bellingham received this news in his cell he asked for a pen and paper and wrote home to his wife:

MY BLESSED MARY,

It rejoiced me beyond measure to hear you are likely to be well provided for. I am sure the public at large will participate in, and mitigate, your sorrows; I assure you, my love, my sincerest endeavours have ever been directed to your welfare. As we shall not meet any more in this world, I sincerely hope we shall do so in the world to come.

My blessing to the boys, with kind remembrance to Miss Stephens, for whom I have the greatest regard, in consequence of her uniform affection for them. With the purest intentions, it has always been my misfortune to be thwarted, misrepresented and ill-used in life; but however, we feel a happy prospect of compensation in a speedy translation to life eternal.

It's not possible to be more calm or placid than I feel, and nine hours more will waft me to those happy shores where bliss is without alloy.

Your ever affectionate,

JOHN BELLINGHAM.

On 18 May, John Bellingham was taken to the scaffold at Tyburn in a cart, which was followed by a large crowd of people who shouted, 'God bless you!' and other words of encouragement to him. A report of his execution said, 'He ascended the scaffold with rather a light step, a cheerful countenance, and a confident, a calm, but not an exulting air. He looked about him a little, lightly and rapidly, which seems to have been his usual manner and gesture, but made no remark.'

John Bellingham died with resignation and dignity, two days after the funeral of the murdered prime minster had been held. René Martin Pillet, a Frenchman who observed and later wrote an account of the execution, described what he felt were the feelings of the crowd: 'Farewell poor man, you owe satisfaction to the offended laws of your country, but God bless you! You have rendered an important service to your country, you have taught ministers that they should do justice, and grant audience when it is asked of them.'

The House of Commons voted to give Spencer Perceval a monument in Westminster Abbey and a substantial grant to his widow and children. John Bellingham's body was taken to St Bartholomew's Hospital, again followed by large crowds. Here, his cadaver was 'privately dissected' for medical research, and his remains were buried in an unmarked grave.

Throughout all of this his wife, Mary Bellingham, had remained loyal to her husband, despite continually trying to persuade him to give up his obsessive campaign. Fortunately, the promises made to John that his family would be taken care of proved true. Mary was indeed financially supported by the people of the town. In fact, the local ladies continued to regularly patronise the millinery business that she ran. This meant that she and her children could continue to live securely, if modestly, in the knowledge that they would always be at home in Liverpool; a town of radicals, of community, and an innate understanding of the need for justice.

WEST KIRBY'S STRANGE BURIAL PLACES

West Kirby is quite a large and delightful village with an attractive promenade that looks across Hilbre Island, nestling at the mouth of the River Dee, towards North Wales. There is much to see and discover in this part of north Wirral, but West Kirby also has its share of curiosities. Not least of these are its two strange burial places; one much more obvious than the other.

Hilbre House, which stood on the coast overlooking the sea at West Kirkby, was the home of John Cummings MacDona (1826–1907), a local landowner, barrister and Member of Parliament (for Rotherhithe, a London constituency), who was also a celebrated breeder of St Bernard dogs.

His favourite dog was 'Tell', largely because the noble animal saved his master from drowning when MacDona was a boy. Tell was also a champion prize winner and when the great animal died, in 1871, at the age of 7, MacDona built a tomb and memorial for his loyal pet at the far end of his garden, looking towards the river. He named the large, circular stone monument 'Tell's Tower'. At its base, and set in a recess behind a detailed life-size carving of the dog, is an inscription that is now badly weathered. This reads:

> Underneath this tower lies 'Tell', the Champion Rough Coated Mount St Bernard Dog of England, and winner of the principal prize of the kingdom since his importation by his owner the Revd J. Cummings MacDona in March 1863.
>
> He was majestic in appearance, noble in character, affectionate in disposition and of undaunting courage.
>
> Died January 22nd 1871, aged 7 years.

Hilbre House, once the home of Selwyn Lloyd MP (1904–78), a senior Conservative Cabinet member, was demolished and a small estate of houses were built on the site. Tell's Tower was incorporated into one of

John MacDona's widow, Mrs Eliza MacDona, at Tell's ornate graveside. (Discover Liverpool library)

The West Kirby Column. (Discover
Liverpool library)

these and, although still visible, is no longer accessible. Apparently, Tell
still lies beneath it.

The second site of interment was never obvious as such at all.
Above Column Road and standing on Caldy Hill at a height of 60ft
is a stately sandstone column surmounted by a large globe set on a
rectangular plinth. In 1841, this was erected by the Liverpool Docks
Trustees (the forerunner of the Mersey Docks and Harbour Board) as
a priority construction project to replace what had stood there before.

This had been a very ancient windmill known as Grange Mill, which
had certainly been standing on the hill since the sixteenth century.
Believed to have been originally erected by a community of monks who
once lived in the district, the old mill was blown down on 6 January
1839, during a severe storm. A report at the time said that it had fallen
'with a great crash', 'breaking its great arms and hurling its stone body

down the hillside'. The millstone landed in the garden of a large house named Kirkland on Village Road – right at the bottom of the hill!

This now caused a major problem for mariners entering the mouth of the River Mersey as for centuries the mill had been used as a navigation aid; hence the urgency to get it replaced by a much more sturdy and appropriate structure. However, when the mill was cleared away and the ground excavated to lay the foundations for the column, a deep chamber was found, cut into the rock, which was full of human bones. They were not laid out in formal burial but piled up in a heap. They seemed to be men, women and some children. They wore remnants of clothing, so were clearly not prehistoric. Because they were in a group this was almost certainly not a plague pit either.

Local people at the time remembered old stories of a gallows once standing near the mill, and speculated that this might have been where they had buried the corpses of executed criminals. Whatever their origin or age, it is said that they were never removed and are still there, beneath the column. The author cannot establish if this is true or not, nor can I find out how many skeletons there were. Nevertheless, the mill stones from the old windmill now form a seat at the base of the column, so when you are next sitting there, eating your sandwiches and drinking your cups of tea – think on!

Rolling Round the World

In 1911, an eccentric but renowned one-armed American came to New Brighton. His name was George Matthew Schilling, who described himself as an American athlete. Standing at a height of 6ft 3in he was powerfully built and, despite his disability, extremely strong. In 1897 he had visited the Wirral seaside resort as just one of hundreds of stops on a global itinerary. He told amazed audiences about a strange marathon challenge that he was undertaking.

Accompanied by his large black dog, named 'King H', he was pushing a 6½cwt wooden globe around the world, from New York and back, to win a bet with an £8,000 prize! This was his second attempt at this feat, as in 1904 he had already achieved this singular goal, also for a bet. The terms of that wager had been that he was required to leave New York with nothing except his globe. In fact, his clothes were made out of newspapers, and he was not to beg, borrow or spend. Also, he was to accumulate the sum of $5,000, which he would keep if he completed the trip. As well as this, however, if his dog died on the journey he would lose half of the prize money. George had won that wager.

Then in 1908, and setting off from London on another bet, he had pushed a large model airship 20,000 miles around Europe, and this had taken him three years. He had won that bet too! Now he was making his new attempt to push his globe around the world, again from and back to New York! Presumably mounted on some sort of wheeled trolley (details are patchy), Schilling's great globe was 7ft in diameter and 22ft in circumference. It had a detailed map of the world painted on the outside. The inside of the globe served as his home, which George had furnished with cupboards for food and general stores, a very comfortable bed, a lamp and a sleeping place for his dog.

To his enthralled listeners in Marine Park at New Brighton he told how he had lost his arm at the age of only 9. It had been torn from his shoulder when he trapped it in a machine whilst working in a factory in his home town of Pittsburgh. So, to make a living, he had begun accepting bizarre challenges and bets. George next told gripping and entertaining tales about his many adventures as he travelled around the world on his current challenge; also giving details of his route.

This had already taken him from New York to Chicago, St Louis and across the Rocky Mountains into Mexico and southern California. Then, from San Francisco he had travelled to Vancouver, where he boarded a sailing vessel and worked his passage to Sydney. Walking through Tasmania and New Zealand, he had next made his way to Japan and China. After passing through Siam and India he walked to Lower Egypt, from where he sailed to South Africa. He had then journeyed to Port Said, from where he crossed through Palestine and Armenia, and on into Russia. Via Austria, Germany and France he had now eventually made it to England and New Brighton!

To raise funds to buy food for himself and King H on his latest 60,000-mile trip, George sold postcards showing himself, his dog and the huge globe on his first round-the-world walk, as well as other

George M. Schilling in 1911, posing in one of his promotional postcards. (Discover Liverpool library)

postcards of him and his model airship. From New Brighton, George and King H simply carried on 'rolling round the world'.

Records of George Schilling's various feats are confusing, but it does appear that he completed this second worldwide walk and, again, won his wager!

MOBY DICK AND LIVERPOOL

From around 1750, until the early decades of the nineteenth century, whaling was a vital part of the maritime economy of Liverpool. Hunting these mammoth creatures for oil, meat and precious and rare ambergris demanded courage, incredible strength and stamina from whale hunters. But, most of all, it required endless patience. Weeks or sometimes months might pass before the water spouts of their prey were sighted. Then the lookout would give the cry that lifted the hearts of the profit-hungry and risk-driven seafarers – 'There she blows!'

Whale oil lit the lamps and lubricated the machinery of the Industrial Revolution (*c.* 1760–*c.* 1830). Whale meat – blubber – was eaten and used in the manufacture of soap and leather goods; ambergris was an essential ingredient in costly perfumes and exotic aphrodisiacs.

However, not all the trips into often dangerous and sometimes icy waters resulted in successful hunts and profitable voyages. The Customs Letter-Books of the Port of Liverpool for 1750 record, 'On the 13th instant arrived the *Golden Lion*, Robert Patterson master, from the Greenland seas, but without any success'.

Whaling ships generally travelled in small fleets, and they would all lower longboats, which the crew would row at break-back speed after the schools of sea giants. In the prow of each of these stood the most important and, after the captain, highest paid member of the crew, the harpooner. It was his responsibility to hurl the heavy, long, barbed spear into the whale with sufficient power to maim and then kill the creature.

The industry reached its peak by 1788, when twenty-one vessels were registered in Liverpool as whalers. In that year this fleet sailed for the Arctic and returned with the oil and blubber from seventy-six whales. Even the hold of a single vessel filled with barrels of whale oil would make its crew, its captain, but mostly its owners, extremely wealthy.

Though profits were great, so too were the risks. Whales frequently escaped their hunters or turned on them and destroyed their longboats and their men. Indeed, in 1789, four whaling ships from Liverpool were lost at sea with all hands. In one famous case, in 1820, the New England whaler, *Essex*, was completely destroyed by a mammoth white whale that sought it out and seemed to deliberately attack it. Only a few of its crew survived. In 2016, the story was told in the film *Heart of the Sea*.

The last permanent whaler operating out of the port of Liverpool appears to have been a ship named the *Baffin*. This was the first whaling ship to be actually built in the port, in 1820, by William Scoresby (1760–1829). However, probably the most significant contribution to the whaling industry came from his son, William Scoresby Junior (1789–1857).

The younger William set sail in the summer of 1822, on a scientific voyage to Greenland. He reported his findings in his book entitled, *A Journal of the Voyage to the Northern Whale Fishery, including Researches and Discoveries on the East Coast of West Greenland made in the Summer of 1822 in the ship the* Baffin *of Liverpool*.

This long and detailed title was a work of great scientific importance, and was essentially a manual on whaling. Nevertheless, despite Scoresby's valuable research, whaling as an industry had declined during this period and by 1827 only the *Baffin* was working as a full-time whaling ship from Liverpool. Even so, Herman Melville (1819–91), the American author, visited Liverpool in 1839 and was so inspired by the wonders of the port, and by William Scoresby's book, that he went on to write his great novel about whaling, *Moby Dick*, in 1851. He also used the disaster of the *Essex* to shape his plot.

Melville tells the tale of the driving and relentless search of Captain Ahab, aboard the whaling ship *Pequod*, for the 'great white whale' after whom the book is named, and which had chewed off the captain's leg on a previous whaling expedition. At the start of the fateful voyage the obsessive captain arouses and exhilarates his men on deck:

'Aye, my hearties … it was Moby Dick that dismasted me; Moby Dick that brought me to this dead stump I stand on now.

'Aye … it was that accursed white whale that razed me; made a poor pegging lubber of me for ever and a day!'

Then tossing both arms, with measureless imprecations he shouted out:

'Aye, aye! And I'll chase him round Good Hope, and round the Horn, and round the Norway Maelstrom, and round perdition's flames before I give him up.

Author Herman Melville.
(Discover Liverpool library)

And this is what ye have shipped for, men! To chase that white whale on both sides of land, and over all sides of earth, till he spouts black blood and rolls fin out!'

In his search for revenge Ahab leads himself, his ship and his crew to destruction in the jaws of his monstrous marine nemesis. In fact, as Moby Dick finally drags Ahab to his death below the waves, the drowning seaman shouts out to the creature, '…to the last I grapple with thee; from hell's heart I stab at thee; for hate's sake I spit my last breath at thee'.

The author of *Moby Dick* had arrived in Liverpool, directly from New York, on his first ever sea voyage and at the age of only 20. He was working as a cabin boy aboard the *St Lawrence*, and he stayed in

Captain Ahab attempts to harpoon
Moby Dick. (Discover Liverpool library)

the port for a month before sailing out again on the same vessel. What he saw and experienced in the town moved, inspired and shocked him, because this crossroads of the world was a melting pot of all nations and cultures and a pool of both great wealth and abject poverty. Ten years later, in 1849, and two years before he wrote his book about the giant white whale, Melville wrote his equally famous semi-autobiographical novel, *Redburn: His First Voyage.*

This tells of a well-educated but naïve and unsophisticated young sailor from New York, named Wellingborough Redburn. Like Melville, the sailor boy is both attracted and repelled by the coarse seafarers, wanton prostitutes and desperate poor people in and around the taverns, brothels, lodging houses and workshops of Liverpool's notorious Sailor Town. His contact with the whaling community in particular would stay with him forever.

Melville himself was overwhelmed by the magnificence of the construction, and the great size and length of Liverpool's docks and the great Dock Wall. Comparing it with the Great Wall of China, he wrote:

> I beheld long, China Walls of masonry; vast piers of stone; and a succession of granite-rimmed docks completely enclosed. The extent and solidity of these structures seemed equal to what I have read of the pyramids of Egypt.
>
> For miles, you may walk along the riverside, passing dock after dock like a chain of immense fortresses.

He was drawn back to Liverpool once again in 1856, when he stayed much longer. Many historians believe that it was Melville who, again in *Redburn*, was the first person to make the connection between Liverpool and the Liver bird, stating that the town had been named after this mythical seabird.

The whaling industry in Liverpool was, for a time, a major contributor to the town's growth. The culture and community associated with the trade also added to the character, as well as the mythology of the port. Nevertheless, by the middle of the nineteenth century, no more whalers sailed from Liverpool in pursuit of great whales, white or otherwise.

HMS *Thetis* – A Floating Coffin

On 1 June 1939, a few months before the outbreak of the Second World War, the Royal Navy submarine HMS *Thetis* was undergoing her sea trials in Liverpool Bay, just off the North Wales coast. Her builders, her crew and the navy were confident that this would be successful and straightforward, but it was not to be.

As she sailed into the bay, and because of an oversight, her No. 5 torpedo tube had been opened to the sea. This would not normally have been fatal except, for a still unknown reason, the torpedo hatch to the inside of the vessel had also been left open. A torrent of water poured in, overpowering all the men inside and making the closing of the hatch impossible. The forward compartments of the submarine flooded, and so she lost trim and plunged bow first to the sea bottom, in 165ft (50m) of water. Nevertheless, the submarine managed to partly resurface with her tail section and rudder sticking up out of the water. However, the rest of her remained submerged, and with the entire crew still alive inside.

All rescue attempts failed and of the ship's compliment of 103 men, of whom fifty-three were her own crew and fifty were technicians and observers, only four men managed to get out through an escape hatch. This left ninety-nine men trapped aboard. The escapees were hauled aboard the destroyer HMS *Brazen*, begging for an urgent rescue of their comrades.

By this time around twenty-six vessels were circling the submarine, crammed with navy personnel, salvage experts and heavy cutting equipment; but they were ordered by the Admiralty to wait and stand off from the submarine. Throughout this time knocking was clearly heard from inside *Thetis*. This was coming from the trapped submariners, desperately wanting to confirm that they were still alive, whilst they waited to be saved.

The men aboard the rescue ships were indeed eager to help those trapped in the submarine, but were still not given permission to do so. Despite their angry pleas, no one explained to them why they could not simply cut through the exposed hull of the vessel to extract the men. As the divers, salvage crews and doctors became increasingly anxious the

HMS *Thetis* and some of the many rescue vessels waiting for permission to assist. (Discover Liverpool library)

So many men were eager and confident that they would rescue the trapped men. They did not know that Admiralty orders would prevent them from doing so. (Discover Liverpool library)

knocking from inside *Thetis* became weaker and less frequent. Before long, it stopped altogether.

After fifty hours trapped inside their submarine in Liverpool Bay all the men inside were dead of carbon dioxide poisoning. They had been killed by the very breath they had exhaled. This is a slow and excruciatingly painful way to die, and HMS *Thetis* was now nothing more than a metal tomb. The deaths of those trapped inside became the Royal Navy's worst peacetime submarine disaster.

Still in the water, but now a floating mass coffin, it was not until 23 August 1939, almost two months later, that a major attempt to salvage the vessel was undertaken. During this operation, which was ultimately successful, Diver Petty Officer Henry Otho Perdue died of a severe attack of the bends, and he will forever be remembered as the 100th victim of the *Thetis* disaster.

On Sunday, 3 September, the same day that war was declared, the submarine was towed to Moelfre Bay, Anglesey, and grounded on shore. Those bodies that had not already been removed by the salvage team were now brought out, to receive a belated naval funeral with full honours. Forty-four of those lost aboard the submarine were interred in a mass grave in Holyhead.

Thetis was soon afterwards taken back to Birkenhead where, after an extensive rebuild, she was recommissioned as HMS *Thunderbolt*. This ill-fated submarine sailed on her first operational patrol on 3 December 1940, but on 14 March 1943, she was depth charged and sunk by the Italian ship *Cicogna*, with the loss of all hands.

It was not until 2009, that details surrounding the *Thetis* disaster became known. It was in this year that previously secret government papers were made public. These confirmed that rescuers could have saved all the trapped men in just five minutes by cutting air holes through the $\frac{5}{8}$in-thick steel hull. A larger hole could then have been cut to release them. The Admiralty had simply refused to allow the rescue because the hull would have been permanently weakened. At that time, and with the Second World War looming, saving the submarine was deemed more important than saving ninety-nine human lives …

After the war, on 7 November 1947, a memorial was dedicated at the gravesite in Holyhead. A memorial plaque to HMS *Thetis* and her crew is also mounted at the foot of the stairwell in the tower of St Mary's Church in Birkenhead. This stands near the medieval priory and overlooks the River Mersey. As one walks up the spiral staircase to the top of the church tower the walls are lined with nameplates, each one bearing the name of one of the lost men, including Petty Officer Perdue. This tribute acts as a stark reminder of just how unnecessary were the deaths of those lost submariners.

STRAWBERRY TEAS AND TOWERS

At the top of William Brown Street (formerly Shaw's Brow), at the heart of Liverpool's St George's Quarter and between St George's Hall and the Walker Art Gallery, stand the Wellington Column and the Steble Fountain. These monuments occupy a triangular plot of land upon which stood a large windmill throughout the sixteenth and seventeenth centuries. Because this was just outside what was then the eastern boundary of the small town, this became known as Townsend Mill.

Just a little further up the hill from this point stood an area named Gibson's Strawberry Gardens. This large, beautifully landscaped garden had a two-storey tea house at its centre, and the whole area had been opened by William Gibson, who was also the manager of the Theatre Royal in the town.

Sometime in the mid-eighteenth century, Mr Gibson had emulated his brother, who had already opened the Ranelagh Tea Gardens on land now occupied by the Adelphi Hotel. These business ventures were very popular and financially successful, making both brothers very wealthy. This was because private pleasure gardens were open to the public for a small admission fee. Such places of refined and 'superior' entertainment suited the tastes and social and cultural aspirations of the new middle classes that were then emerging in Liverpool.

The entrance to the Strawberry Gardens was located at what was then the junction of Shaw's Brow with the road now known as Islington. This was a narrow country lane with fields and gardens on both sides. It was originally called Folly Lane as it led to Gibson's Gardens.

The reason why this name began to be applied to the Strawberry Gardens was because of the action taken by Gibson following a disagreement with Liverpool Corporation. Things were going so well for Mr Gibson that he decided to increase the length of his tea house and widen the area of his gardens, but the Corporation denied him permission. Undaunted, and refusing to miss out on the increase in profits he expected from extending his premises, Gibson decided to build up instead of down. This led to the construction of a broad, square eight-storey tower adjoining his existing tea house.

Despite the fact that local people took to naming the tower 'Gibson's Folly', this new attraction proved very popular with them.

Gibson's Folly, in the heart of his Strawberry Tea Gardens. (Discover Liverpool library)

They delighted in being able to climb the winding stairway right up to the top. From here they had spectacular views of the surrounding countryside and of the river. This provided an exceptional opportunity for people to see their town, literally from a new and thrilling perspective, and Gibson made even more money as a result.

Access to what had also now become known as the 'Folly Gardens' was through a wooden door in a surrounding fence, then through a turnstile where the admission tickets were sold, and along a shrubberied pathway that led to a tavern. The Folly Gardens not only produced strawberries, but also had damson, apple and pear trees, and it was a popular delight to come and pick the fruit at the rate of 'a penny a piece'! There were also two bowling alleys in the gardens, as well as a skittles alley and, just outside the gardens, an ancient and popular cock-pit. Like his brother's Ranelagh Tea Gardens, Mr Gibson also had a large fish pond in the centre of his grounds. This was surrounded by a fine lawn on which were situated a number of long benches, where visitors could sit, especially on summer evenings, to chat, smoke and drink a speciality beverage called 'Braggart' – a mixture of ale, sugar, spices and raw eggs.

The following report of a boyhood mishap in the Folly Gardens describes an incident that took place around 1780:

> I used to sail a model ship on the pond in the Garden, made for me by the mate of the 'Mary Ellen'.
>
> I one day fell in, and was pulled out by Mr Gibson himself, who fortunately happened to be passing near at hand. He took me in his arms, dripping as I was, into the tavern and I was put to bed while a man was sent down to Church Street, to acquaint my parents with my disaster, and for dry clothes.
>
> My mother came up in a dreadful fright, but my father only laughed heartily at the accident, saying he had been overboard three times before he was my age. He must have had a charmed life, if he spoke true, for I don't think I could have been above eight years old then. … After I got dry clothes, Mr Gibson took us up to the top of the Gazebo or look-out tower. The view was magnificent. We could see Beeston Castle quite plainly, and Halton Castle also, as well as the Cheshire shore and the Welsh mountains.

In 1780 the Townsend Mill was demolished, and in 1785 so were the tea house and its tower. The Strawberry Gardens were also swept away and the whole site was cleared, levelled and paved over. It is unclear why this action was taken, but I suspect that Mr Gibson had upset the Corporation again!

By 1790, the former gardens had become the location for an annual open-air festival and carnival known as the 'Folly Fair'. This public event, of course, had been named after Gibson's tower, and it was held each Easter Monday and Tuesday. The grand event soon became an eagerly anticipated and popular attraction, drawing in people from across the town and surrounding communities. Booths were erected all over the area, from which traders and merchants sold all kinds of goods and novelties, as well as food and drink; the gingerbread seller's booth was always particularly crowded.

There were also temporary theatres, merry-go-rounds and swing boats, whilst singers, dancers, musicians, acrobats and puppet shows all kept the crowds amused and excited. Wrestling matches were held in the surrounding fields and the fair gradually extended up Folly Lane (Islington) as far as Prescot Street.

However, the Folly Fair became particularly well known, not to say notorious, for the 'lifting' competitions held there. Each Easter Monday the men would attempt to lift up any local women who happened to be in the vicinity, and on Easter Tuesday the women would attempt to do the same with the men. This led to the fair becoming infamous for lewdness and rowdy behaviour. The respected local historian and architect, Sir James Picton (1805–89), wrote at the time that Folly Fair 'became a saturnalia of the lowest roughs in town. Drunkenness, debauchery and fighting prevailed to a frightful extent'.

After a number of failed attempts by the local police to close it down, in 1818 Liverpool Corporation issued a licence for the Islington Market to open on the site. This forced the fair to move to a new location in what is now Stafford Street off Islington. Its popularity quickly declined and, around 1820, the Folly Fair finally passed into history, along with the Strawberry Gardens and Gibson's Folly.

CRYPTS, CATACOMBS AND CORPSES

On the summit of St James's Mount stands Liverpool's Anglican cathedral, which is the fifth largest in the world, and was only begun in 1904. At the left side of the main drive into the cathedral stands a small, neoclassical building called the Oratory. Now a repository for some of the works from the city's collection of sculpture, this was built by the then town architect, John Foster Junior (1786–1846), as a mortuary chapel. It was in this building that services were held for those about to be interred in the massive, sunken cemetery at the base of the Mount, known as St James's Burial Ground, and which Foster also designed.

This deep and very large graveyard had previously been a great quarry gouged out of the earth over centuries. Records referring to it go back as far as 1572. Stone from here was used to build many of Liverpool's famous older buildings, such as the Town Hall, as well as in the construction of many of the dock walls of the port. By 1825, though, the quarry was exhausted and it was decided to convert it into an Anglican cemetery. Work began in 1826, and Foster designed it as a 'city of the dead', modelled on the Père-Lachaise cemetery in Paris.

The new cemetery was needed because the rapidly expanding population of the town was by this time causing major sanitary problems, one of the most pressing being the lack of public burial space. The only other public cemeteries at this time were the burial grounds at what is now St John's Gardens, behind St George's Hall, which had opened in 1767, and the Necropolis at Everton (now Grant Gardens), which had opened in 1825.

The St James's Burial Ground helped to alleviate some of the problem, however, by the early decades of the twentieth century and after 57,774 burials, it was found that every time a new grave was being dug old bones from previous burials were being disturbed. It was obvious that the cemetery was full so, in 1936, it was closed and redeveloped as a public park. All of the bodies were left where they lay but most of the gravestones were re-sited to line the walls of the old quarry.

Today, between the Oratory and the great cathedral, through a tall iron gateway, a steep, narrow pathway winds its way down to the bottom of the burial ground. This passes through a short tunnel carved out of the rock by the first quarry workers. This was once the footway in and out of the workings but it is now the entrance into the graveyard. This pathway is lined on both sides by ranks of old tombstones. These stand like ominous sentinels, with the names of the long dead still legible and reminding us that we too shall one day join them.

On entering the former burial ground the first things that can be seen are the great ramps and terraces that zig-zag across the far wall. These were created when the old quarry was closed, for funeral carriages and hearses to access over 100 rock-cut catacombs. Most of these are sealed shut with their cadaverous contents locked inside, but some, just a few, remain open and empty as if waiting to yet fulfill their purpose.

As well as being the final resting place for many thousands of ordinary people, the mortal remains of a number of significant citizens of Liverpool also lie buried here. These include John Foster Junior himself, who was not only the architect of the cemetery but also of many of the city's outstanding buildings and docks. Here also is the grave of Edward Rushton (1756–1814), who was blind and had been a sailor, a journalist, a poet and a human rights campaigner. He was also the founder of the Liverpool School for the Blind, which was the first such school in the world. Here also lie members of three families, each of whom were related to victims of Jack the Ripper!

William Lynn (1792–1870), who was one of the founders of the Grand National, rests here, as does Captain William Harrison, who died in 1860, and was the first master of the magnificent, transatlantic paddle steamer the *Great Eastern*. He drowned in a tragic accident, when the small boat carrying him and some crew members from the huge ship to the mainland capsized in a sudden gale in Southampton Water. Also, two of Admiral Horatio Nelson's officers are buried here, each of whom lived to be over 100 years old.

Infant mortality was always high in Liverpool and standing against the wall at the bottom of the entrance path to the cemetery can be found a particularly pitiful row of tall tombstones. These formerly marked the burial places of children from the old Bluecoat School and

St James's burial ground, now a public park and gardens. (Discover Liverpool library)

other orphanages in the town centre. The stones list the names and the very young ages of dozens and dozens of children. These include one boy named 'Oliver' and another named 'Twist'. Charles Dickens (1812–70), the great Victorian novelist, visited Liverpool many times. He even worked a shift or two as a special constable in a dockside bridewell as part of his researches. Perhaps the burial ground also provided him with inspiration ...

Groves of old trees entirely shroud the base, walls, paths and carriageways of the cemetery. Their branches form a vaulted canopy above a number of still standing gravestones and monuments. The whole place is tranquil yet mysterious even by day, as the sunlight is broken up by the leaves and limbs of the tall trees, and as they cast interchanging fingers of light and shadow across the graves. Flowers bloom and shrubs thrive between the burial places, and birds sing as the great cathedral gazes down in protective splendour.

An allegedly healing spring opens up in the far wall, spilling into a small pool near the tall, circular mausoleum of William Huskisson

MP (1770–1830). He was run over and killed by the *Rocket* steam locomotive on the inaugural run of the Liverpool to Manchester Railway, and so became the world's first railway fatality.

At night though, it may be that the cathedral is the power that keeps some unquiet spirits at bay in the cemetery, because there are many reports of ghosts and spectres manifesting in the silent night-shrouded stillness. Indeed, the entire cemetery can be eerie and disquieting at night time, as grasping claws of moonlight now break through the trees. The whole scene is then lit by creeping ribbons of silver. But these can be quickly driven away by the enshrouding clouds that suddenly pitch everything into darkness, and not all the souls that lie here are quietly at rest.

The burial ground is regularly visited by groups of enthusiastic ghost hunters. They report that around the Huskisson mausoleum can be heard disembodied but heavy footsteps. These seem to circle the tomb and, sometimes, the faint shape of a tall man can be seen, dressed in Victorian clothes and drifting across the pathway. Could this be the shade of the unfortunate politician?

They say that the figure of a woman can sometimes be seen near a bench at the base of the terraced catacombs, where she holds her head in her hands and softly weeps. As she does, an equally spectral breeze ruffles the folds of her white crinoline dress and the ribbons of her bonnet. Also, a number of people have told the author, with conviction, that near the tombstones of the orphans can be heard the plaintive weeping of a child, lost, alone and wandering. Such tales leave us in no doubt about our own mortality. But, the cathedral, the trees and flowers, and the daytime sunlight that lights this most unusual of public parks and gardens, reminds us too that there is hope and that death is just another chapter in the story of our existence.

The Birthplace of 'Being Prepared'

In 1876, Robert Baden-Powell (1857–1941) went to India as a junior army officer and soon specialised in training young soldiers in scouting, map-making and reconnaissance. His methods were unorthodox for the time but they were very successful. This was due particularly to his use of small units or patrols, working together under one leader and with special recognition for those who did well. For proficiency, 'B-P' (as he had become known) awarded his trainees badges resembling the traditional design of the north compass point. Later he served in Africa during the Boer War (1899–1902) and helped defend Mafeking during its 217-day siege.

The courage and resourcefulness shown by the boys, aged between 12 and 15, in the Corps of Messengers at Mafeking made a lasting impression on him. In turn, his own deeds made him a national hero in England, when he returned home in 1903. He also found that the small handbook he had written for soldiers, *Aids to Scouting*, was being used by youth leaders and schoolteachers all over the country to teach observation and woodcraft.

This gave Baden-Powell plenty of food for thought, so from 31 July to 9 August 1907, he took twenty-two boys, aged 9–17 and from very different social backgrounds, on a ten-day camp on Brownsea Island, in Poole Harbour, Dorset, to test out ideas he was formulating for a new national youth movement. The activities he organised worked so well and made such an impression on the boys that B-P was ready to put his plans into wider action. However, he realised that he needed to organise and mobilise if he was to achieve his goals.

So, he decided to go to one of the most deprived, yet energetic, parts of Britain to speak about his ideas for a national 'Boy Scout' movement, and so he came to the North. He also needed a town with a large population of teenage boys, who he knew would have the will, stamina and imagination to respond to his call. This also needed to be a place where he would also find adults with the necessary skills and qualities to lead these young boys – this is why he came to Birkenhead.

On 24 January 1908, in the YMCA building that once stood on Grange Road in the town, B-P gave a speech to a large, enthusiastic audience and the response was exactly what he had hoped for. Around the same time, he published his manual for Scouting called *Scouting for Boys*. This came out in six fortnightly instalments, between January and March 1908.

This caught the national imagination, and Boy Scout troops were established right across Britain and, before long, the world, all now

Poster advertising the 1929 Boy Scout Jamboree at Arrowe Park in Birkenhead. (Discover Liverpool library)

adopting B-P's own motto to 'be prepared'. The rest, as they say, is history.

So it was that the true beginnings of the international Scouting movement began in Birkenhead over 100 years ago. Because of this, in 1929, Birkenhead Borough Council was asked to host the International

Scout Jamboree on the 21st anniversary of the movement. This was held at Arrowe Park from 31 July to 13 August 1929, and it was an outstanding success. Over 50,000 Boy Scouts and Girl Guides attended from over seventy countries, and there were more than 300,000 visitors. This event remains the largest Scout Jamboree ever held and, once again, it was in Birkenhead!

HARTLEY'S VILLAGE – A SWEET COMMUNITY

The Industrial Revolution (*c.* 1760–*c.* 1830) forever changed the face and fabric of Britain, and of Merseyside – physically, architecturally, politically and culturally. A new breed of powerful and wealthy industrialists were reshaping industry, manufacturing and commerce, and this impacted on ordinary people in an unprecedented way. In their tens of thousands, people began to move from the rural countryside, seeking work and opportunity in new manufacturing towns and great ports. This mass migration now transformed these places into rapidly expanding urban conurbations.

Like ancient Rome, all roads led to Liverpool. This was already one of the world's greatest ports, the crossroads of the world and the most important town in the British Empire outside London. More often than not, though, the 'land of milk and honey' that these desperate people were hoping to find was simply a place of disillusionment, grinding poverty, disease and premature death. The conditions of the time also meant that they encountered political and economic exploitation, as the rich certainly became richer, and the poor inevitably got poorer. Britain became a much more polarised society as a result, especially in towns like Liverpool.

But, it was not all bad news. Not every wealthy capitalist was an exploitative, profiteering villain; some had noble ambitions to use their wealth for the greater good. Many built schools, hospitals, orphanages, museums, libraries and churches. Others established charitable foundations, whilst some created entire, largely self-contained villages for their workers.

These were designed to provide good quality housing and other facilities such as education, healthcare, community centres, gardens and sports fields, as well as organised community events and social activities. They also included such rare amenities as gas and electricity, lavatories, sewerage systems and plumbing with running water.

The driving forces behind such developments were usually the religious faith and political ideology of their creators, bolstered by a paternalistic outlook that was so prevalent amongst the wealthy in Victorian and Edwardian Britain. As a result, these men imposed strict rules, standards of behaviour and codes of morality on their workers and their families, and they expected total compliance and obedience in return for their charity. They also recognised that they would get higher productivity, and therefore greater profits, from a happier and more grateful workforce, so they were rather more like benevolent dictators than entirely selfless altruists. Nevertheless, workers in these specially constructed neighbourhoods certainly did benefit from a higher standard of living and quality of life, as well as from a sense of secure community in a very insecure world.

This meant that throughout the history of the Industrial Revolution and its immediate aftermath we see the establishment of such model communities as Bourneville. From 1893, this was created by the chocolate manufacturing Cadbury brothers of Birmingham. We also see the building of Saltaire in Yorkshire, in 1851, by Sir Titus Salt (1803–76), the great textile mill owner, and from 1888, Port Sunlight on the Wirral, by the soap magnate William Lever (1851–1925), Lord Leverhulme. However, one of the lesser known of these patriarchal communities was established by the jam manufacturer, William Pickles Hartley (1846–1922), at Aintree in Liverpool.

Born in Colne in Lancashire, William Hartley began his life as a grocer. In 1871, as a result of one of his suppliers failing to deliver a consignment of jam, he decided to make it himself. This proved to be a great success and was very popular with his customers. In fact, so many other retailers were now buying his tasty jams that he decided to increase production. In 1874, he opened a large factory in Bootle, just north of Liverpool. However, he found that this did not have the transportation links he needed to ensure fast and reliable delivery of fresh ingredients for his preserves, or for the rapid distribution of his finished products to his increasing network of customers. So, in 1886, he moved his entire operation to a new factory in Aintree. Designed by the Derbyshire-based firm of Sugden & Sons, Hartley had his new plant built in red brick, and with external medieval styling, including turrets, so that its main entrance looked like a castle. He also erected an impressive, tall, ornate, red-brick clock tower at the heart of his complex.

He next laid railway lines directly alongside his factory buildings and, when the trains arrived, they did so on the tracks of the Cheshire Lines and the Lancashire & Yorkshire Railways. These brought fresh fruit and vegetables from farms and orchards all over the three counties. The raw ingredients were then immediately unloaded onto conveyor belts, manually sorted into varieties, and checked for the high quality and freshness that Hartley insisted upon.

The conveyors then carried the produce inside the building, where it was washed, cooked and made into varieties of jams and other preserves. These were then transported out on the same railway lines and sold all around the world. Hartley's commitment to high standards and good value guaranteed the success and sustainability of his business, and the Aintree factory provided secure employment for around 1,200 men and women. Many people still remember with affection the factory at its peak of operation. They also miss the smell of fresh fruit and baking jams that settled over Aintree like a warm, sweet, reassuring blanket.

Just like the other enlightened Victorian and Edwardian entrepreneurs Hartley was determined to see to the wellbeing and character-building of his employees. Whilst he was a successful capitalist, William also had strong socialist leanings and he believed in the necessity and 'rightness' of bringing management and labour closer together. These attitudes were driven by his Christian faith and membership of a thriving Primitive Methodist congregation, as well as by his lifelong hatred of alcohol.

William Hartley paid generous wages to all his employees and provided them with a full pension scheme, as well as access to a factory doctor and basic healthcare. Hartley also believed in profit sharing, and each year he divided these out amongst all of his workers at the rate of 15 per cent of their wages.

In the same year that he opened his Aintree factory, William married Mary Horsefield, the daughter of a fellow grocer from Colne.

They went on to have seven daughters and one son. Mary shared her husband's religion and philosophies, and the couple immediately decided to give 10 per cent of their annual income to charities. As their wealth increased so did the level of their donations, rising to 15 per cent, and then to 20 per cent. In his later years, William set aside a third of his annual income as a fund to continue to provide donations to good causes and deserving cases.

Like his fellow benevolent industrialists in other parts of Britain, Hartley also wanted to create a model residential community for his workers. And so, in 1888, 'Hartley's Village' was officially opened, adjacent to his large factory complex. Although initially providing only forty-nine houses for a core group of his most skilled workers, Hartley's Village had many of the same elements that could be found at Bourneville, Saltaire and Port Sunlight. Also designed by Sugden & Sons, the houses were built to the highest standards, in sandstone and the same red brick as his factory. However, they were of contemporary, utilitarian design, rather than medieval. An article in *The Builder* magazine, published in the same year, stated, '[The architects] have designed the cottages in conformity with the old domestic buildings indigenous to the district and avoiding all flimsy and supposed

Hartley's Jam Factory, original main entrance.
(Liverpool Athenaeum library)

"picturesque" ornamental additions – for which they are entirely to be commended.'

The houses ranged in size from 'two up, two down' terraces to small semi-detached houses and larger detached properties. The size of house you lived in depended on your job status in the factory, so the managing director and his family lived in the largest detached house.

A number of the original streets survive, and the broadest was the main street of the village, named Hartley Avenue. Off this ran streets named after the ingredients of jam: Sugar Street, Spice Street, Red Currant Court, Cherry Row, etc. They were all broad and spacious and had large alleyways behind them, each at least 12ft wide. The rents that Hartley charged for the houses were very reasonable, running at between 2s 6d and 3s 6d a week. Some were also available for sale on twenty-year mortgages at low rates of interest. All the surviving properties are now privately owned.

Many of the houses were grouped round a central 1-acre bowling green which, sadly, is now a car park. Tennis courts were also laid out, and there was a sizeable fishing pond for the village, which was stocked with carp, roach, rudd and large goldfish (these were always returned to the water after being caught).

Sports days, tournaments, outings and celebrations were a regular feature of life in this happy community. Many of these were organised by factory management and others by the workers and villagers themselves. People were proud of their homes and village amenities and they took care of these, as well as of each other. Hartley's Preserves continued to thrive, and more houses were either bought or built for factory employees, including some on nearby Cedar Road, bringing the total available to seventy-one.

Hartley also built the Aintree Primitive Methodist Chapel on Cedar Road and, in 1896, a temperance meeting hall and café known as the Aintree Institute. Standing on Longmoor Lane in Aintree, Hartley founded this as a place where 'all the churches, from the Roman Catholic Church and the Church of England, down to the smallest mission room ... enter into a Christlike compact to fight evil in every form'. In later years the institute became a social club and music venue where the Beatles performed thirty-one times. Sadly, in 2006 the building was demolished.

In 1891, Hartley was honoured in Parliament when a report was presented by the Board of Trade. This stated:

> The preserve factory of Mr. W.P. Hartley of Liverpool has always sought to maintain good relations with his workforce. His factory is a model to all. The arrangements indicated an employer who has been anxious that his prosperity should rebound to the well-being of his workforce, by joining profit sharing.

In 1903, William was awarded a knighthood in recognition of his philanthropy. In fact, during his lifetime it is estimated that, as well as his creation of the village and benevolence to his workers, Sir William Pickles Hartley gave away at least £1 million.

After living in Liverpool for forty years, he retired to Southport where, in 1922, he died at the age of 77. He was buried in his home town of Colne, where he had also made many contributions and donations to charity, including the building of the Hartley Hospital. He was honoured there just as much as he was in Liverpool.

In 1891, Hartley's jam factory expanded significantly, and did so again, in 1899. It was extended further in 1923, the year after William Hartley died. The Hartley Company continued to operate, but it was taken over, in 1959, by the American Schweppes company. Over the following decade the preserves production operation at Aintree was wound down, and the Hartley Jam Factory was soon moved to a more modern facility in Cambridge.

Hartley's factory and village were not at first considered to be of any historical or sociological significance, and were therefore unprotected from developers. So when the factory was finally closed down in the 1970s, parts of this and the village were subsequently demolished. This included the magnificent house named 'Inglewood', which had been built as the home for the factory manager. Much of the remaining factory site was built over and redeveloped as small retail, wholesale and factory units. This was not done sympathetically, and the whole area around the village now looks rather sad and neglected, as does the surviving medieval-styled factory entrance.

When, around this time, it was discovered that plans were afoot to demolish the magnificent clock tower, a campaign to save it was organised by the remaining villagers and other supporters. Despite their strenuous efforts, however, this glorious example of late-Victorian, neo-Gothic architecture was also pulled down, in 1977. This was yet another demonstration of the architectural and cultural vandalism so prevalent across Merseyside in the closing decades of the twentieth century.

Although the Hartley name and monogram can still be seen all over the village and on what survives of the factory buildings, for a long time the achievements of William Hartley went largely unrecognised in Liverpool. Also, the remaining factory buildings were allowed to fall into decay and dereliction. Fortunately, and at long last, the Grade II listed buildings that still comprise Hartley's Village and factory were, in 2011, declared a Conservation Area of 'special architectural and historic character'. It is reassuring to know that the enthusiastic organisation, the Hartley's Village Heritage Council, continues to fight to keep William Hartley's memory alive and his legacy maintained.

OLDER THAN STONEHENGE – THE CALDER STONES

The Calderstones district of Liverpool and the magnificent public park that sits at its centre take their name from the Calder Stones. These are six, prehistoric, irregular-shaped sandstone megaliths that once formed part of the Calderstones chambered tomb. This was a Neolithic chief's tumulus, or burial mound, that had been erected around 4800 BC. That means that this ancient structure and its standing stones was older even than Stonehenge, which was built around 3100 BC. Stonehenge itself is even more ancient than the pyramids of Egypt, the oldest of which is the stepped Pyramid of Zoser, which was constructed around 2600 BC.

The Calder Stones appear to have originally stood as part of the entrance to the central burial chamber. There were originally more of them, although the exact number is not known. Inside the main tomb other tall stones would have supported a roof and at least two walls right at the heart of the tumulus, and were known as dolmen. It was here that important members of the community would have been ceremoniously interred by local tribespeople. This was used for more than one burial over a period of many years and was the likely focus of important religious ceremonies.

From the Middle Ages, when the district began to be farmed and inhabited, local people largely ignored the burial mound and the standing stones that showed through the top of it (except for stealing some of the smaller stones now and again for building!). Between 1760 and 1790, the large mound of sand that remained as partial cover for the tumulus and its stones was carted away to mix with mortar for building a nearby house called Woolton Lodge, long since demolished. When all the sand had been removed, a rough stone chamber was exposed, inside which were a number of plain, clay burial urns. These contained a large quantity of dried bones. Sadly though, late eighteenth-century Liverpudlians had no sense of history and many of the urns and their contents, as well as some of the smaller standing stones, were simply scattered around the nearby fields.

The Calder Stones and tomb are first noted in a map from 1568, when they formed part of the boundary between the manors of Allerton and Wavertree, but they had been known and named for centuries before this. The name 'Calder' is derived from the Celtic word '*galdar*', or 'wizard', and baseless legends told how the stones had been the focus of mysterious rites and rituals carried out by ancient Druids. People whispered of virgins being sacrificed with golden sickles and their bodies pierced by sticks of mistletoe.

Fortunately, in the early nineteenth century the burial site attracted the attention of local archaeologists and scientists, who began to seriously excavate, investigate and research it. They reported:

> ... in digging about them, urns made of the coarsest clay, containing human dust and bones, have been discovered, there is reason to believe that they indicate an ancient burying-place.
>
> When the stones were dug down to, they seemed rather tumbled about in the mound. They looked as if they had been a little hut or cellar. Below the stones was found a large quantity of burnt bones, white and in small pieces. There must have been a cart-load or two.

At least not all of the artefacts had been lost to posterity!

Whilst the archaeologists were very interested in the tomb chamber itself, it was the large standing Calder Stones that especially excited them, because these encircled the entrance and had clearly been deliberately marked and carved into a variety of shapes.

Sometime later the nearby road was being widened, so scientists took advantage of the opportunity to dig once more into the burial mound. This time they found more stones, but these were found to have beautifully detailed and clearly visible carvings on their surfaces, of spirals and 'cup and ring' marks and also hand and footprints, some with extra fingers and toes! There are many similarities between the artwork on the Calder Stones and that found on tombs dating from the same period in Wales and Ireland. This suggests that people from these three areas were in contact and shared the same beliefs. Neolithic axes, arrowheads and pottery shards have been found all over Liverpool, particularly in Toxteth, West Derby, Woolton and Wavertree. However, the markings on the Calder Stones are unique, which makes them of particular European significance.

Despite these more accurate Victorian interpretations of the origins of the stones, the Druidical association had become embedded in local

The Calder Stones in their original location, *c.* 1905, but rearranged and fenced in. (Discover Liverpool library)

mythology. In 1845, Joseph Need Walker (1790–1865), who then owned the Calderstones estate, fully accepted that local legends about bloodthirsty Druid rituals were true, especially as the ancient stones had 'obviously' been erected in a sacrificial circle. Consequently he rearranged all the stones in a rough circle of his own design and built a low wall with railings to surround them. Perhaps bowing to good taste, rather than laying a sacrificial slab at the centre of the circle Walker planted a fir tree!

The Druid connection persisted well into the twentieth century, and when new roads were being laid out close to the stones these were named Druids Cross Road, Druidsville Road, Druids Gardens and Druids Park.

In 1954, Liverpool City Council decided to remove the stones for cleaning and preservation. This was a major operation that took the labour of nine strapping men with a low loader: the largest stone weighs around 3 tons, and even the smallest weighs around 5cwt. Even so, they did the job in only a day, and moved all of the Calder Stones to a private council maintenance yard within Calderstones Park. Only six of the large standing stones now survive, and in 1964, these were moved to their present location in the purpose-built glass 'vestibule'

The Calder Stones inside their display greenhouse
in 2016. (Discover Liverpool library)

conservatory building. This circular greenhouse structure stands in the Harthill section of the park and, although permanently locked up, the great stone slabs can be clearly viewed through the windows.

However, at the time of writing plans are currently underway to re-site the Calder Stones more sympathetically. They will be positioned as much as possible in their original layout, but in a much more accessible area in the grounds of the Calderstones Park Mansion House, originally built for Joseph Walker in 1828. Members of the public will then be able to see, study and learn about Liverpool's most ancient site and one of Britain's most important archaeological relics – much older than Stonehenge!

DINGLE – A HAVEN OF ROMANCE AND BEAUTY

On the flanks of the Toxteth Ridge, which is one of the seven hills of Liverpool, the urban district known as the Dingle sits on a sandstone cliff. This once fell sharply away to the riverbank, but no longer, although it still overlooks the River Mersey and the Wirral. To people from Liverpool who are familiar with the area, what is now a densely populated post-industrial fringe of the inner city seems to be seriously misnamed. This is especially true because the reputation and history of parts of the neighbourhood was once one of economic depression and social breakdown: 'Don't go down the Dingle – that's were de kids play tick wi''atchets!'

Previously, though, this had been an isolated and entirely rural part of the ancient Toxteth Forest. But in the mid- to late nineteenth century there was a rapid influx of thousands of manual workers who moved into the district seeking work on Liverpool's vast expanse of docklands. These people settled in hundreds of streets of newly built terraced houses that were then spreading across Dingle.

Despite this, and even as late as the 1890s, all of the land between Park Road and the Mersey certainly deserved its idyllic name. Before industrialisation this was a broad area of largely isolated mansions surrounded by sizeable private estates and gardens. There were also clusters of small estate workers' cottages that nestled on the river's edge. At the end of the eighteenth century, in a guidebook to Liverpool,

Dingle was described as being 'A paradise in the North … One of the most beautiful places in the district … a sweet, romantic dell, planted and laid out with considerable taste.'

Even later, in 1843, another guidebook said:

> A sweet romantic dell … It is a delightful retreat, extending to the river, having all the diversity of hill and dale, wood and grove, tastefully laid out in shady and winding walks, with numerous arbours and rustic seats. Few persons in Liverpool are aware of the beauty of this romantic spot … Admission is gratuitous, visitors only being required to enter their names in a book at the lodge, to prevent improper persons gaining access to the ground.

Allow me to further paint the scene for you:

As warm summer afternoons blended into balmy evenings, and whilst the sun began its steady descent towards the far horizon, the Dingle Brook and other streams skipped and gurgled their merry dancing way across the rural and rustic scene. The woodlands were filled with birdsong as the branches of the trees broke up the sunlight into a carpet of mottled, shimmering gold on the grass below. Groves of shrubs, bushes and wildflowers added colour and shaded mystery to the scene, all spread out along the top of the sandstone cliff. Young courting couples strolled hand-in-hand through the sylvan scene, filling their lungs with sweet, fresh air. Hidden from view in the thickets of laurel and rhododendron, they would tenderly kiss and plight their troth, caressed by soft breezes from the great waterway and the sea beyond, all swathed in the heady perfumes of Mother Nature.

In the rocks around which the trees and shrubs grew was a small cave, named by the locals as the 'Old Time Alcove'. This was believed to be the home of the mythical spirit of the woods and waters there, known as 'the Lady of the Dingle'. She was often seen in the twilight, flitting gracefully and ethereally through the foliage.

The great radical, poet, author, slavery abolitionist and politician William Roscoe (1753–1831) wrote a famous poem about her called *The Nymph of the Dingle*:

Once the maid, in summer's heat, careless left her cool retreat,

And by sultry suns opprest, laid her wearied limbs to rest;

Forgetful of her daily toil, to trace each humid tract of soil,

From dews and bounteous showers to brine the limpid treasures
    of her spring.

In 1790, Roscoe retired to a cottage in the Dingle, on a site that became twentieth-century tram sheds at the top of Aigburth Road.

The Dingle cliff ended in a sheltered cove known as Knott's Hole. This was a natural basin that provided a safe and secluded pool, scattered throughout with large boulders and almost completely encircled by a wall of sandstone that was about 15–20ft high. The pool was fed by the Dingle Brook, which had given the district its name and ran down through the district from high on the ridge. It meandered its way down towards the Mersey along what is now High Park Street, although the brook had widened to become a small creek by the time it cascaded over the edge of the cove onto the small sandy beach and the river below.

The Dingle Glen and brook in the 1900s. (Discover Liverpool library)

This attracted boys and young men from the nearby communities, from the town itself and often from as far away as Edge Hill. They came to leap and dive from the cliffs and boulders, and to swim and play in the clean, clear waters of the Mersey. However, the Reverend Thomas Spencer drowned whilst bathing in Knott's Hole in 1811.

In 1808, the Dingle estate was purchased by the Reverend John Yates (1755–1831), a Unitarian minister, who enhanced its natural beauty with planting and landscaping. In 1821, he sold the western part of the estate to James Cropper (1773–1840), a Liverpool merchant, Quaker and slave trade abolitionist. Cropper now created his own estate, which he named Dingle Bank. Around 1823, he built three large houses for members of his own family as well as the workers' cottages on the shore.

The Croppers were influential people who moved in the most intellectually illustrious circles. Indeed, amongst their renowned visitors were Harriet Beecher Stowe, the author of *Uncle Tom's Cabin*; Josephine Butler, the Victorian feminist and campaigner on behalf of prostitutes; and Mrs Humphrey Ward, the eminent Victorian novelist. A frequent guest was Matthew Arnold, the poet and cultural commentator, who actually died in the Dingle, in 1888, whilst visiting his sister, Susan Cropper. The local primary school is named after him.

For many decades the estate owners had opened up their lands, a couple of evenings every week, to allow and indeed welcome members of the public to come and enjoy what was a delightful, almost Arcadian setting. But time marched on, and so did industrialisation. By the beginning of the twentieth century the whole district had developed into complexes of docks and wharves, as well as into estates of houses for the thousands of workers now toiling along the length of the riverfront. Dingle Brook dried up and its old watercourses were then used as sites for drains and sewers. The lease of the entire Dingle estate was bought by the Corporation of Liverpool, who allowed the tipping of household rubbish, ash and industrial waste in and around the shoreline, and the whole area was completely ravaged and destroyed.

An iron foundry and a ship-breaking yard had also been established on the river bank, and waste and pollution from these so discoloured a long stretch of riverbank that it became known locally as 'the Cast Iron Shore', or 'the Cazzie'. This remained a popular playground for local children until the 1980s.

In 1919, the Dingle cliffs and riverfront had been acquired by the Mersey Docks and Harbour Board. They immediately demolished the remaining isolated mansions and all the cottages. They replaced these with oil jetties, petrol storage tanks and chemical ponds. They also built a river wall that wiped out Knott's Hole and soon the railway came through the area. Also, parts of the Dingle became a post-war dump for rubble and masonry from buildings destroyed in the May Blitz of 1941.

In 1984, however, the now empty chemical tanks, overfull industrial dumps, long abandoned oil jetties and silted up docks of the Dingle were also swept away in their turn, when the entire area was reclaimed and recreated as a fabulous collection of gardens and modern houses, named the International Garden Festival. A new road, Riverside Drive, was created through the site, and the location of Knott's Hole is now covered by a small traffic roundabout on the approach to the Britannia pub, which was also built in 1984.

However, a section of the cliffs at Dingle Point still overlooks the pub and roadway. This, together with the recent re-landscaping and restoration of Festival Gardens and the Otterspool Promenade and parkland, means that we can now imagine what pre-industrial Dingle once looked like. We can also discover a delightful place to come and relax and play once again.

The Wailing Widow of Liscard Castle

On the Wirral, in the small town of Liscard in Wallasey, is Seaview Road. Here once stood a grand stately mansion house that had been built in 1810, and officially named Marine Villa. This was the home of John Marsden (1793–1853) and, in fact, Seaview Road was originally known as Marsden's Lane.

Marsden made his money from the brushes and brooms that he manufactured, and his products must have been in great demand because he became very wealthy and built the huge, neo-Gothic structure for himself, in the style of a mock medieval fortress. Local wags first nicknamed it 'Broom Castle', after its builder's profession, but to counteract this Marsden renamed his horse Liscard Castle. This suited the very large and grand house because of its tall turrets, crenellated roof and mullioned windows. High above the main entrance and set in the pediment between the two main turrets was a great carved stone lion that added to the grey stone structure's imposing facade.

Nearby Castle Road and Turret Road originally took their names from this building, but the building was demolished, in 1902. This was only after it had stood abandoned and overgrown for some years, and after passing through the hands of a number of owners, none of whom had lived there for long, apparently because of the ghost! This was after the house had been subdivided into three separate homes, named the Castle, the Turrets, and the Towers, but still, no one ever lived happily on the site, which many local people are still convinced is haunted.

The story goes that a handsome sea captain and his beautiful young wife moved into Liscard Castle sometime in the latter half of the nineteenth century. One day, the mariner bid an emotional farewell to his wife and set sail on what was to be a long sea voyage. Apart from a cook and a housemaid his young wife was left alone in the rambling and rather soulless stone pile. Without children she was lonely, and wandered the large rooms of the house pining for her husband, anxious for his safety and unable to shake off a feeling of terrible dread that something was wrong. Then came the awful news that her husband's ship was reported to have foundered and that her husband had been lost at sea and presumed drowned.

The bereft young woman was distraught, and prowled the rooms of her house repeatedly crying out her husband's name and wailing most piteously for her lost love. So much so that she was often heard by passers-by. Eventually, she could take it no more and late one stormy night she wandered outside into the large area of open land that surrounded her house, where Hose Side Road now stands. Here was a large water-filled pit and, unable to face life without her husband, she threw herself into the deep water and drowned herself, calling out as she did so that she was going to rejoin her husband. This pool afterwards became known as Captain's Pit.

Not long afterwards, a workman was brought in to work in the building, following complaints of mysterious knocking sounds coming from its cellars. He had been instructed to seal up some old tunnels that had been discovered leading deep under and away from the house, but he soon ran screaming from the building and nothing could persuade him to return. When, much later, he had calmed down, the builder reported that he had seen and heard the spectral figure of a young woman, dripping with water and approaching him with wide, mad, staring eyes and her mouth agape and wailing.

It was said that for years afterwards the drowned widow's tortured cries could be heard around the large house, and that from time to time she could be seen about its corridors and rooms, tearing her hair in grief and stretching out her empty arms in anguish. Even today, there are reports still of the ethereal wailings and sobbing cries of a young woman swirling around the area, especially in the dark of night.

Liscard Castle just prior to its demolition.
(Discover Liverpool library)

SEA SHANTIES, MAGGIE MAY AND 'WOMEN OF EASY VIRTUE'

SEA SHANTIES

Shanties were the work songs sung by the crews of wooden, square-rigged vessels during the great age of sailing ships; especially those that put out to sea from the Mersey to ports around the globe. The rhythm of the songs helped the sailors keep a steady pace when working on board ship, especially when turning a capstan or as they hauled ropes and raised sail.

The word probably derives from the French word '*chanter*', meaning 'to sing', and the sailor who led the singing was known as the 'shanty man'. He sang the main lines or verses of the song whilst the hauling gang would join in on the choruses, making each haul on the rope, or turn of the capstan as they did so. Shanties were generally only sung aboard British, American and Canadian vessels though, as some Continental countries did not approve of singing at sea!

Shanties began in the fifteenth century and continued through into the twentieth, but they are not used very much today as work songs because almost everything is automated and mechanised on modern ships. Nevertheless, they are still much loved by modern sailors and sung by them and folk musicians. Traditional shanties can be grouped into a number of main types:

Short haul shanties – for jobs that only need quick pulls over a short time, usually hand over hand.

Halyard, or long-drag shanties – for heavier and longer pulls, generally with a short break to rest in between verses.

Pumping shanties – sung when men had to pump water that had collected in the bilges as a result of leaks – all wooden ships leaked!

Capstan shanties – smoother songs for long, repetitive tasks that needed a sustained rhythm, but not involving working the lines. As the name implies these were mainly sung when turning capstans to haul up the anchors.

The crew below decks, joining in a rousing fo'c'sle sea
shanty chorus. (Discover Liverpool library)

Fo'c'sle shanties – these were not work songs at all, but just sung for fun
and entertainment during long and often tedious ocean voyages.

Liverpool, as a seafaring town, is the source of hundreds of such
shanties and fo'c'sle songs, particularly associated with the port –
such as 'Blow the Man Down', which mentions Paradise Street in
particular, 'Heave Away', 'Oh You New York Girls' and 'The Leaving
of Liverpool':

> Farewell to Princes' landing stage; River Mersey fare thee well;
> I am bound for Californ-i-a, a place I know right well.
> So fare thee well my own true love, And when I return united we will be;
> It's not the leaving of Liverpool that grieves me, But my darling when
>   I think of thee.

MAGGIE MAY

Of all the sea shanties associated with Liverpool and the Mersey,
one of the most famous is 'The Ballad of Maggie May'. Maggie was
a 'woman of easy virtue' – a prostitute who worked Paradise Street,
Peter Street and the docksides of early nineteenth-century Liverpool's

Sailor Town. She became internationally known and notorious, hence the song.

The earliest reference to this particular shanty appears in the diary of Charles Picknell, who was a sailor on the convict ship *Kains* which, in the 1830s, sailed from Liverpool to Van Diemen's Land, which we now know as Tasmania. This is the large island off the Australian mainland where, during the eighteenth and nineteenth centuries, the British government maintained six penal colonies. These were for prisoners who had been sentenced to 'transportation' for a variety of crimes, ranging from petty theft to brutal assault.

However, the most notorious penal colony was on the Australian mainland at Botany Bay. Many men, women and children found themselves sailing out of Liverpool on convict ships bound for such places of long and grim exile. As, seemingly, did Maggie May.

Maggie certainly did exist, and is believed to have had rooms at 17 Duke Street. She also plied her trade out of the Crown pub and the American Bar on Lime Street, and was known for robbing the sailors she took into her bed. The sea shanty tells her story:

> Oh! I'll never forget the day when I first met Maggie May,
> She was standing on a corner at Canning Place,
> In a full-sized crin-o-line, like a frigate of the line,
> And as she saw I was a sailor she gave chase.

> She gave me a saucy nod, and I, like a farmer's clod,
> Let her take me line abreast in tow,
> And under all plain sail, we ran before the gale
> And to the Crow's Nest Tavern we did go.

> Next morning when I woke, I found that I was broke,
> No shoes or shirt or trousers could I find,
> When I asked her where they were, she answers 'My dear sir,
> They're down in Lewis' pawnshop number nine.'

Whilst the full song says that she was a thief who took advantage of the matelots who crossed her mattress, this was not generally true of Liverpool prostitutes. Indeed, especially during the nineteenth century and early decades of the twentieth, when poverty, neglect and disease were rampant in the town, most of these women were simply poor girls, resorting to the only commodity they had left to sell to feed themselves, and often their children too.

But it was not just Maggie who worked Lime Street and the port's taverns and rooming houses and who became renowned. Others were Mary Ellen, known as the 'Battleship'; 'Jumping Jenny'; 'Tich' Maguire; 'the Horse'; and 'Cast-Iron Kitty'! These were just a few of the many women who provided a particular kind of companionship for sailors far from home, up and down Liverpool's streets and in and out of its inns, taverns, and rooming houses.

'The Ballad of Maggie May' has been sung in pubs, on street corners, at gatherings and at ceilidhs all over Liverpool and beyond for over 150 years. But what of Maggie? Well, the song says it all:

Oh Maggie Maggie May they have taken her away
And she'll never walk down Lime Street any more.
For the judge he guilty found her,
Of robbing a homeward bounder,
An' now she's servin' time in Botany Bay.

Versions of the original ballad have been recorded many times over the decades, including by Judy Garland, in 1964, and the Beatles, in 1970.

That prostitution was rife in the Liverpool of those days is undeniable; just as it was in every other sea port and major city across Britain and the world. And like life's other inevitabilities, death and taxes, it will always be with us – but no longer on Lime Street, perhaps!

The Star-Crossed Lovers of Wavertree Hall

One of Liverpool's many claims to fame is that it was the home of the world's first school for the blind. As mentioned previously, this was opened in 1791, by a remarkable sailor, poet, journalist, human rights campaigner and slavery abolitionist by the name of Edward Rushton.

In 1898, the school moved from a site in Hardman Street to a new building on Church Road North in the Liverpool suburb of Wavertree.

It was constructed on the site of Wavertree Hall, which had possibly once been the family seat of the important and wealthy Perceval family, who claimed descent from Viking invaders in the tenth century.

In the mid- to late nineteenth century, Wavertree Hall had been held by another wealthy family and, in 1865, the daughter of the house, Margaret, fell in love with the family's coachman, whose name was Edward Murphy. The coachman was young, tall, handsome and virile, with a muscular body, dark hair and pale blue eyes, so it is easy to see why the young girl would have fallen for his undoubted attractions.

Margaret knew that her martinet of a father, the local squire, would never approve of their relationship, and not just because Murphy was working class – a bad enough crime in Victorian England – but because he was also Irish and a Roman Catholic! In the eyes and prejudices of the squire, such a relationship was absolutely impossible, so the young couple eloped in secret.

When he discovered what his only daughter had done, Margaret's staunchly Protestant parent was outraged. So much so that he immediately wrote her out of his will, and ordered that the gates to the grounds of the hall be permanently locked and the path to the front door ploughed up, so that she 'could never return home'. These instructions were actually written into the deeds of the property and they are still in force today.

The star-crossed lovers are believed to have spent some time in Ireland where, because Margaret was a Protestant, they were also rejected by Edward's Catholic family, so they returned to Liverpool, where they lived in great poverty in the Scotland Road area of the town.

However, there is a footnote to this unusual tale. In February 2011, I met Julia Lisman, the great-granddaughter of the coachman, and she verified the details of the story. Julia also told me that the couple had a son, also named Edward, and that Margaret's mother, entirely unknown to her husband, regularly and secretly visited her daughter in their poor home and provided her and her family with gifts of money and food to keep them from the workhouse.

Julia believes that their child, her grandfather, Edward Murphy Junior, was born sometime around 1870, and died in the early 1940s. Whatever the nature of his origins, Julia's family now also believe that he went on to establish a printing business in Liverpool named the Eldon Press, and that he also became a typesetter with the *Liverpool Echo*.

But what of the gates to the former Wavertree Hall? Following the strict rules of the lease they stand there still, in the main wall of what is now the Royal School for the Blind. The gates were restored in 1955, but they remain permanently locked and the pathway is still grassed over. A new gateway and entrance path had to be cut to allow the family to enter their home, and this is the one the school still uses today.

The permanently locked gates of the former Wavertree Hall. (Discover Liverpool library)

EVERTON VILLAGE CROSS AND 'OLD NICK'

The cross of old Everton village had probably stood in the centre of the village green since the sixteenth century. It was still there when the Everton lock-up was built in the eighteenth century and was an important feature in the tightly knit community.

The cross consisted of a round pillar about 4ft high that stood on three square stone steps, and it had a sundial set into the top. The cross was much treasured by the people because it had helped to save the villagers' lives during outbreaks of the plague. This dreaded pestilence had afflicted the Liverpool area many times, especially during the seventeenth century, and when it came to Everton the cross had taken on an entirely new significance.

The villagers accepted a self-imposed quarantine and left money in bowls of water on the steps of the cross. This enabled local farmers to visit the village green once the people had gone back into their houses. They then exchanged the 'clean' money for food and supplies. The farmers and traders from outside the village did this regularly until the plague passed. In this way the tradespeople remained uninfected and, fortunately, many Evertonians survived.

As the years passed, and by the beginning of the nineteenth century when the village was becoming busier and more populous, the stone cross became something of a traffic hazard. This was especially true in the dark of night, when people, carts and horses frequently collided with it, and it was proclaimed a nuisance by the local gentry. Even so, the Evertonian villagers refused absolutely to allow it to be removed or re-sited.

Then, in 1820, on a dark, windy, rain-battered stormy night, all the villagers were tightly locked up against the elements inside their homes. But when they awoke in the morning they found that their cross had vanished – sundial, pillar, stone steps and all. Nothing at all was left to show it had ever stood there. Where had it gone? Who had taken it?

As far as the villagers were concerned there was only one possible, reasonable and likely explanation: Old Nick, the Devil himself, had obviously caused the storm so that he could come and spirit the old monument away simply to upset the people of Everton. This tale spread

The Everton village cross. (Liverpool Athenaeum library)

beyond the village, right across Liverpool. Soon people came from all over to see 'the cross that wasn't there', and to ply local villagers with ale in the local taverns so that they could be told colourful tales of demons and devils and storms. The truth, as ever, was much more prosaic.

An influential local gentleman by the name of Sir William Shaw had become so fed up of regularly crashing into the cross himself that he decided to take action in secret. He paid two men with a wheelbarrow, picks, shovels and spades, under the convenient cover of the storm, to remove the cross piece by piece. They hid the disassembled stones in the village lock-up, in the middle of the green. Then, over successive nights, the pieces were stealthily taken out of the lock-up, carted away from the village and dumped.

It was many years before the truth came out, but for generations afterwards people still insisted that the Everton village cross had been stolen by Satan.

Scrimshaw, Scuttlebutt and 'Shiver My Timbers!'

Liverpool has always sat as a hub of the world's maritime trade and as the 'crossroads of the world' for people and commodities. The city developed its own culture, community and dialect; each influenced by the sea and the people who sailed upon it. The language and customs of these intrepid seafarers has left a legacy in the many descriptive words, phrases and expressions that are now commonplace in our everyday conversation and communications. However, the original meanings of these, as well as the fact that they were first used at sea, are now generally forgotten. Here are just a few, perhaps surprising, examples:

Aback – To be startled or disconcerted.
This comes from the nautical term that describes a ship sailing into an often sudden strong wind, so that she cannot make any headway.

By and large – Generally speaking; on the whole.
To sail 'by and large' is to do so close to the wind and slightly off it. This makes it easier to steer the ship and so prevent her being 'taken aback'.

To Shanghai – To drug and abduct.
To Shanghai someone is to get them insensibly drunk, or to drug them, so that they can be abducted into forced service aboard ship, especially to the China Seas. This possibly originated on the Liverpool waterfront in seamen's taverns like the Baltic Fleet. Many an unwary matelot might have a soporific or 'Mickey Finn' slipped into his tankard of ale by a villainous 'crimp'. He would later wake to find himself aboard a ship at sea bound for the Chinese port of Shanghai.

Scrimshaw – Ornamental carving on debris.
This word describes small pieces of wood, bone or seashells that had intricate designs of images carved into them by sailors who had time on their hands whilst at sea. The term is believed to come from a man named Scrimshaw who was particularly skilled at the artform.

You can whistle for it – You won't get what you want.
This comes from a time when superstitious sailors believed that when their ship was becalmed on the ocean they could call up a wind by whistling. However, this could be risky and they might not get what they wanted, because whistling aboard ship was considered to be the music of the Devil. This meant that they might actually whistle up Old Nick in the form of a gale and so wreck their vessel.

With its carved picture this early nineteenth-century piece of walrus tusk becomes a piece of scrimshaw. (Discover Liverpool library)

Scuttlebutt – Rumour or gossip.

From the early nineteenth century, the barrel or 'butt' of fresh drinking water on board ship was the place around which sailors would gather to chat, and to exchange news and information. Today we might call this a 'water cooler conversation'! The word 'scuttle' originally meant to put a hole in the butt so that water could be drawn from it. This word also means the deliberate holing of the hull of a ship so that she would sink.

The Seven Seas – All the seas of the world.

This term actually references oceans rather than seas, and are the Arctic and Antarctic, the North and South Pacific, the North and South Atlantic, and the Indian Oceans.

Ships of the line and ratings – The size and quality of warships; the best and the less so.

A 'ship of the line' was a warship that was sufficiently well-armed to take her place in a long row for an attack, or 'line of battle'. This technique of warfare at sea was developed from the mid-eighteenth century when battleships were divided into three categories:

1   First Rates – vessels of three decks carrying at least 100 cannon.
2   Second Rates – ships of three decks with 90 cannon.
3   Third Rates – two-decked vessels with either 64 or 74 cannon on board.

This latter ranking led to the general term 'third rate', meaning 'not the best', with 'first rate' obviously being the very best.

Turn a blind eye – To tactfully pretend not to notice, or to deliberately overlook something.

At the naval Battle of Copenhagen in 1801, Horatio Nelson (1758–1805), who was then vice admiral, was sent a flag signal from the ship of the fleet commander, Admiral Sir Hyde Parker (1739–1807), ordering him to disengage from the battle. However, Nelson is said to have disregarded the signal by putting his telescope to his blind eye and saying that he had not seen it. The great naval hero then went on to be victorious in what was a very hard-fought combat with the Danish Navy.

Shipshape and Bristol fashion – Neat, orderly and organised.

A sailing ship that was properly and efficiently rigged, well stocked and equipped was said to be 'shipshape'. To also be 'Bristol fashion' was to be the best-rigged vessel, based on the fact that Liverpool's great rival port had a reputation for excellence in this regard.

Shiver my timbers! – An expression of disbelief or surprise.

The word 'shiver' in this sense means to 'shatter' or 'split into pieces', and the phrase was used as a swearing term by sailors on board ship. Their 'timbers' in this context being their bones; as in the strong, main wooden braces that made up the skeleton of their vessels.

A tight ship – To be efficient and disciplined.
Literally, a ship in which the ropes, rigging and all the sails are tight, trimmed and ready for action. To 'run a tight ship' is therefore to run an efficient ship.

Show a leg! – Get out of bed!
This was shouted out by officers to wake up sailors and to quickly get them out of their beds or hammocks, 'Wakey, wakey, rise and shine, the morning's fine; show a leg, show a leg, show a leg!' This comes from the days when the wives (and sometimes the mistresses) of seamen were allowed to sleep on board ship. To make sure that it was only the men who got up, as the women were allowed to stay in bed, the shape and amount of hair on a leg would indicate the gender of its owner – although not in every case, of course.

Son of a gun – A light-hearted, generally manly greeting.
What became a term mostly used in American westerns actually originated aboard British sailing ships. When the pregnant wives or lovers of sailors went into labour aboard ship, they would usually have to deliver their babies behind the cannon. If the child was unable to be given a name, because its father failed to admit to it, then the birth would be entered in the ship's log as a 'son of a gun'.

Swinging the lead – To be idle, or try to get out of doing work.
This comes from a 'leadman' on board ship, whose job it was to take depth soundings using a lead weight on a long length of cord. This was considered an easy job and so appropriate for a lazy sailor.

Three sheets to the wind – Very drunk.
A 'sheet' on board ship is actually the rope attached to the clew of a sail, and which is used for 'trimming' or tightening the sail. If the sheet is not taught then the sail will flap 'in the wind' and so will the sheet. This makes the ship unsteady at sea. On board ship, and in the dockside taverns, to be 'a sheet in the wind' is to be 'a bit merry', whilst 'three sheets' is to be falling down drunk, or 'legless'!

Ships that pass in the night – A chance acquaintance that is unlikely to reoccur.

This comes from a line in a poem by Longfellow – *Tales of a Wayside Inn, III*, 'The Theologian's Tale – Elizabeth', written in 1874:

> Ships that pass in the night, and speak to each other in passing,
> Only a signal shown and a distant voice in the darkness;
> So on the ocean of life we pass and speak to one another,
> Only a look and a voice; then darkness again and a silence.

OLD MOTHER RILEY, THE BOXING KANGAROO AND WILD WILLIE WEST

In Argyle Street in Birkenhead once stood the Argyle Theatre. This was opened on 21 December 1868, originally as the Argyle Music Hall. Part of the building also contained a fully equipped billiard room, a luxurious lounge and eight 'American bowling alleys', each 70ft long. The cost of the entire 'entertainment complex' was £10,000.

Also known as the Argyle Theatre of Varieties, in 1876 it changed its name to the Prince of Wales Theatre, staging dramas and other productions as well as lavish pantomimes. But, in 1890, it reverted to its original name and also to offering full bills of music hall entertainment.

Even though the theatre only had seating for 800 people, in the main auditorium as well as in two galleries, the Argyle was one of the most famous and renowned music halls outside London. Indeed, some of the world's greatest performers considered the small, provincial theatre important enough to want to perform here. These included such stars as Dan Leno, Arthur Lloyd and a very young Charlie Chaplin, as a member of the clog dancing troupe known as 'The Eight Lancashire Lads'. Popular Liverpool comic George Robey, 'the Prime Minister of Mirth', appeared a number of times, as did Vesta Tilley, famous for her song 'Burlington Bertie'.

Stan Laurel performed at the Argyle before he met Oliver Hardy. Flanagan and Allen sang 'Underneath the Arches', and Irish washerwoman, Old Mother Riley (alias Arthur Lucan), with Kitty McShane, had audiences in gales of laughter at her antics.

Argyle Theatre

BIRKENHEAD.

Manager - - D. J. CLARKE.

Two Performances Nightly, at 6-50 & 9.
MATINEE every Thursday at 2-30.

MONDAY, May 29th, 1905,

HOUDINI

WEE MONA
BOSTON TWINS
J. W. RIGBY
ANNIE MYERS
LILY RAMSDALE
CHAS. AUSTIN

THE BREWSTERS

The Orchestra under the direction of
Mr. E. DENNEY.

POPULAR PRICES.

Popular Scots singer Harry Lauder, and famous escapologist Harry Houdini both appeared at the Argyle. (Discover Liverpool library)

George Formby Senior was very well received, but not so his son, George Formby Junior. His performance did not satisfy the Birkenhead audience so he was booed off the stage! Harry Houdini 'road tested' some of his greatest escape stunts at the theatre and other American artistes who appeared were W.C. Fields and the original 'Three Stooges'.

The theatre proclaimed itself to be 'the cradle of the stars', and Sir Harry Lauder began his career at the Argyle, in 1894. Morecombe and Wise also appeared there as very young entertainers. Nor should we forget Billy Scott-Coomber and his Singing Grenadiers, Dainty Doris, the Sparkling Mozelles, Leoni Clark's celebrated Boxing Kangaroo and Wild Willie West.

Unfortunately, because of the influence and magnificence of the many great theatres in the powerful city of Liverpool across the water, the Argyle's importance and achievements are often overlooked. In 1896, the first moving pictures to be shown in England, outside London, were shown here in the form of 'Thomas Edison's Vitagraph Living Pictures'. Electric lighting was specially installed for the occasion and the Argyle was one of the first theatres to do so.

One of the bandsmen aboard *Titanic* was John Clarke, formerly a bass player with the orchestra of the Argyle Theatre. He died with his fellow musicians when the ship struck an iceberg in 1912 and sank with the loss of over 1,500 lives. He and his fellow musicians continued to play as the ship went down in an effort to keep up the morale of the doomed passengers. Contrary to common belief, the last song they played was actually 'Song of Autumn', not 'Nearer My God to Thee'.

Some of the earliest BBC radio broadcasts were made live from the theatre including, on 14 April 1931, the first ever broadcast of a music hall show, which was heard across the British Empire. On 14 March 1935 the first ever live music hall broadcast to America was also made from the Argyle.

But then, at the height of the Second World War, on 26 September 1940, the theatre took a direct hit from a German incendiary bomb. The resulting fire completely gutted the auditorium leaving only the shell of the building. This remained standing but neglected until 1973, when it was finally demolished. The site is now a pay and display car park.

At the time of writing, nowhere in or near the site of the outstanding and important old theatre is there even a commemorative plaque, let alone an information board to remind the people of Birkenhead of the significance and pioneering role played by the Argyle Theatre. I remain optimistic that before long this is an oversight that will be rectified.

THE DOCKERS' UMBRELLA

Merseyside has always been the home of much that is unique and revolutionary. A perfect example of this was Liverpool's Victorian elevated railway. By the mid-nineteenth century the traffic at the entrances to each of the docks, and around the surrounding roads along the full length of the working riverfront, had reached such a state that terrible congestion occurred on a regular basis. Apart from men with carts or barrows, all road traffic at that time was horse-drawn. This frequently brought transportation and commerce to a noisy and frustrating halt. These were Liverpool's first traffic jams, but of vehicles, passengers and animals.

The blockages were also making it difficult for the thousands of dockers to get to work, not just on foot but by horse-drawn omnibuses and trams. Some method of relieving the problem was urgently needed. In 1852, the Dockside Light Steam Railway was installed to transport goods the entire length of Liverpool's docks. Running alongside the Dock Road, this passed every dock gate. Passengers were also carried along the railway in specially designed horse-drawn, broad-wheeled omnibuses that could run either on or off the tracks. However, this did nothing to relieve the still increasing traffic problem.

The idea of an overhead railway had been proposed as early as 1853, but nothing had come of this. But, by 1878, the level of Dock Road congestion had become so intolerable along what was then more than 6 miles of docks that the plan was revived. This was immediately approved by the Mersey Docks and Harbour Board and the Overhead Railway Company was formed, in 1888. Construction of the imaginative transportation system began the following year and it was built to run directly above and following the route of the existing steam railway.

Beginning at Herculaneum Dock, at the southernmost end of the docks system, the Liverpool Overhead Railway was intended to carry specially designed engines and carriages along what had now grown to 7½ miles of the Liverpool Docks system. At first, it had been intended to use steam locomotives, despite the experience of New Yorkers where, from their elevated railway, burning cinders, ash, oil and hot water were regularly raining down on the heads of the people walking below. Fortunately, this idea was rejected once it was also realised that falling sparks could ignite the timbers of the hundreds of wooden ships moored at the docksides. Consequently, in 1891, a system of electric traction was commissioned from the newly formed Electric Construction Company.

The first overhead train ran in 1892, carrying all the company directors and their friends and families. Then, in February 1893, the new railway was officially opened to the public by Lord Salisbury, as the world's first elevated electric railway. With trains running in opposite directions on two parallel tracks this was also the first electric elevated railway in the world to use an automatic signalling system.

What soon became locally known as the 'Dockers' Umbrella' ran to Seaforth Sands at the north of the city, where a purpose-built elevated station was constructed. In 1921, Britain's first escalator was installed here. This consisted of a narrow conveyor belt with wooden slats on which the passengers stood. The handrail was fixed, though, so using this was a bit of a challenge! At Herculaneum Dock the station was at ground level and the tracks and carriages were accessed up a staircase, as was the case at all the other stations.

The railway track ran 16ft above the Dock Road and the journey took twenty-five minutes, serving seventeen stations. The new transportation system proved to be instantly popular and commercially successful, and very soon it was carrying over 4 million passengers every year.

Herculaneum Dock was filled in, in 1980, and over it now stand modern apartment blocks and a sports and fitness centre. Behind these, the great sandstone Dingle cliff towers above the buildings and nearby Riverside Drive. Halfway up the rock face a large porticoed archway can clearly be seen. Although now partially bricked up, this shows the point at which a railway tunnel emerges over the former dock and *under* streets of terraced houses on the cliff top. This tunnel was for an extension to the Overhead Railway, continuing the line from Herculaneum Dock to an underground station at Park Lane in the Dingle. Opening in 1896, the extra 1½ miles of track then provided a new community of thousands of workers with direct access to their places of employment.

Serving all the docks and warehouses, as well as the complexes of light and heavy industry along the riverfront, this transport system became vital to dockers and industrial workers alike. The track also passed by the city centre at the Pier Head, and so it served the office workers in buildings such as the Cunard and Royal Liver buildings. This meant that the railway also provided access to the heart of the

A poster advertising the fun and thrills to be had aboard the
Dockers' Umbrella. (Discover Liverpool library)

city itself, and to its retail and commercial centres. As well as this, passengers on the Mersey Ferries could connect with the Overhead at the Pier Head Station, and people could simply travel on it as a cheap, convenient and fascinating mode of transport for an entertaining outing.

However, having been badly bombed during the Second World War, and suffering from severe acid corrosion from pollution and salt corrosion from the sea and river, by the late 1940s the Overhead Railway had become very dilapidated. Also, the steam from the Dockside Light Railway, which had continued to run at ground level directly below the elevated track, had rotted, rusted and destabilised the ironwork of its rails and supporting stanchions. By the beginning of the 1950s its condition was giving cause for grave concern. In post-war Britain money was not available to adequately repair the railway or to bring it up to the required safety standards, despite the fact that it was still carrying almost 9 million passengers every year. Consequently, the Overhead was closed on 30 December 1956, and subsequently demolished in 1957, following sixty years of successful operation.

In its final year, when I was 5 years old, my mother took me for a trip along the full length of the railway. She was determined that I should have the opportunity to travel on the Dockers' Umbrella just once before it disappeared forever. I remain very grateful for this experience and I clearly remember gazing down on the docks as we clattered above. I can still picture what appeared to be hundreds of ships sailing on the river and berthed in all the docks. I remember crowds of people, of all shapes, sizes and skin colours, walking the length of the Dock Road.

I remember, too, the masculine smells of oil, sweat and Capstan Full Strength cigarettes from all the men who filled the carriage in which Mum and I sat, reassuringly reminding me of my Dad. I recall, too, the sounds of the strange accents of the sailors and workers from all over the world, and of the rattling and shaking as the wooden carriages trundled along the clanking and ringing metal track. Even today, the excitement and thrill of it all is a vivid and happy memory.

All that now remains of the Overhead Railway are some of the lower track support girders, set in concrete mounds standing against some stretches of the Dock Road wall. However, the complete underground station area at the Dingle still remains, deep inside the cliff under the streets of houses. But the platforms, ticket office and the signal box have long gone, as have the tracks and the trains, and the whole underground station area became the workshop for a large car repair company.

The full length of the Dingle Tunnel still exists, leading all the way to the tunnel mouth above Herculaneum Dock. A few years ago I walked this tunnel in the pitch dark, past the old railway sleepers and avoiding the water that drips down through the roof from the bedrock above. I climbed a ladder against the wall that blocks off the lower part of the tunnel mouth and gazed across the sports centre and the apartments, across the car showrooms and the Chinese restaurant and out above the river to the Wirral. This was another remarkable experience that complements the one I had as a small boy.

What an asset such a public transport system would be today, had the Dockers' Umbrella survived. All we can do now, though, is breathe a sigh of regret as we look back on what was an engineering marvel, and once one of our greatest social and economic assets. Unless, that is, Peel Ports continue with their development plans for the Liverpool waterfront. As the owners of the bulk of Liverpool's (and the Wirral's) docks, locks, quays and warehouses, they have a grand vision for the complete regeneration of the largely derelict north and central waterfront. This will create 'Liverpool Waters', a spectacular complex of towering offices, apartments and leisure facilities. They are also speculating about building an elevated monorail to carry passengers above the streets from Stanley Dock, along the riverside and Dock Road, all the way to Liverpool John Lennon Airport at Speke. So, who knows? Perhaps a twenty-first-century version of the Dockers' Umbrella will return to Liverpool – we can hope …

THE PUNCH AND JUDY PEOPLE OF MERSEYSIDE

Richard Codman was born in 1832 in Norwich, of Romany origin, and was taught the skills of woodcarving, music and puppetry by his father, George (1811–92). As a young man Richard wanted to explore the country and so he travelled to the north-west, via Birmingham and

Wales, giving shows with puppets and dogs at markets and fairs along the way.

By 1860, he had arrived in Llandudno, where he collected driftwood from the shore, which he then carved into a set of traditional Punch and Judy show characters. Many of these are still owned by his descendants. Right away Richard began giving puppet shows on the beach, under the banner 'Professor Codman's Wooden Headed Follies' and, from that time, the family have regularly performed their puppet shows at this Welsh seaside resort.

Records tell that the Punch and Judy show first appeared in Britain after the Restoration of King Charles II in the seventeenth century, when the country wanted fun and frolic again after decades of misery under Cromwell and the Puritans. The comic story had evolved from the tale of 'Punchinello', which originated with the medieval Italian '*Comedia del Arte*' street theatre troupes. Soon, travelling puppet shows became quite a feature of the British way of life. Originally using string puppets called marionettes, the characters evolved into the much more practical and portable glove puppet characters that we know today because this was much easier for itinerant, single showmen.

Richard also used glove puppets and, by 1868, he had made his way to the port town of Liverpool. Here, he immediately approached the Corporation for permission to give public shows. They were delighted by the idea of a traditional Punch and Judy show in their town so they granted him a performers' licence. They also gave him a permanent pitch on the Quadrant. This was in the middle of Lime Street, at St George's Place, directly opposite the front of Lime Street Station.

Richard Codman died in 1909, by which time his son, Richard Codman II, born in 1870, had taken over the family business. By the 1920s the show had become so popular and such a feature of Liverpool life that a new puppet booth was hand-carved by the famous local sculptor, H. Tyson Smith. This new miniature theatre was formally presented to Richard in 1922, by the Sandon Studios Society at a special ceremony held in the Bluecoat Chambers Arts Centre, and the Codman family continue to use this booth today.

When Lime Street was redeveloped in 1957, the Codmans' magnificently ornate, colourfully dressed and painted puppet theatre booth was re-sited to stand on St George's Plateau. The frame, with its proscenium arch, was left on the plateau between performances and it was never vandalised!

By the late 1960s, traffic around St George's Hall was so busy that it became dangerous for crowds of people to cross to the plateau to watch the shows. The council then moved the Punch and Judy show to a new regular pitch in Williamson Square, with the theatre booth then stored in the nearby Playhouse Theatre. This was a highly appropriate association, as the large theatre and the very small one had both continued to play an important role in Liverpool's cultural heritage.

The Codman family had used the same traditional script for their show since first coming to Liverpool, just changing some characters and topics to suit the times and contemporary ways of life. This included a puppet version of Ken Dodd saying how 'tickled' he was and how 'tatifalarious' it was to be there!

As a boy in the late 1950s, the author watched the Punch and Judy show often, and got to know the storyline well; which was actually very violent. It featured wife beating, baby battering, an incompetent and violent policeman, a hanging, a haunting and an encounter with the Devil. Still – all good, clean family fun!

The plot of the show had been significantly debrutalised by the beginning of the 1970s, but the performances were still exciting, unusual, lively and very, very funny. There was the popular 'Look out he's behind you!' scene, with the ghost. This always provoked enthusiastic audience participation from both adults and children. There was also the mischievous Joey the Clown, who was the only character who managed to outwit wily Mister Punch. He was based on the famous real life Victorian clown, Joseph Grimaldi (1778–1837).

But a highlight of each performance was Mister Punch's encounter with the crocodile. The reptile was determined to eat Mister Punch, who simply reached down the monster's throat and pulled out a long string of sausages, loudly squeaking 'That's the way to do it!' in triumph. The uniquely distinctive voice of Mister Punch is a cross between a squeak and a growl. This is produced by the use of a 'swazzle'. This flat, round miniature kazoo is placed at the back of the puppeteer's throat and is only ever used for the voice of Mister Punch. It has risks attached, though, because if the puppeteer is not skilled in its use he can either swallow it or choke – very unpleasant in either case.

Professor Richard Codman III with Judy and Toby, the dog, in his booth on Lime Street. (Courtesy of Professor Richard Codman III)

Punch always has a stick, of course, representing the 'slapstick' of traditional travelling street performers and Victorian music hall artists. This was two strips of wood tied together at just one end, so that even when struck against somebody very lightly it would produce a very loud 'smacking' sound, making the blow appear much worse than it actually was.

During every performance, sitting placidly at the end of the stage or 'playboard', sat Toby the dog, who had also been a traditional character in Punch and Judy shows since early Victorian times. Each incarnation of the very much alive animal was trained to sit still, wearing a brightly coloured ruff around his neck and interacting with Mister Punch as part of the performance.

Richard Codman II died in 1951, and Richard Codman III, who had been born in 1897, then took over the Punch and Judy mantle. He was the 'Professor', who entertained my parents, my brother and me, the rest of the city and Merseyside throughout much of the second half of the twentieth century. When he died in 1985, I was particularly saddened. This was because I had got to know him very well from my boyhood and he had fuelled my own interest in glove puppetry. He had also advised me on the design and building of my own Punch and Judy theatre booth and had helped me set up my first part-time business, as a teenaged travelling puppeteer.

Richard's son, Ronald Richard, was born in 1928, and died in 2015, and he became the next Professor Codman. It was Ronald Richard who entertained my own children over the years. From 1860 to the present day, five generations of Codmans have given their puppet shows across the region, whilst other members of the family have maintained their Llandudno pitch.

One of the family's first proscenium arches and some of their puppets are now on display in the Museum of Liverpool at Mann Island – a permanent reminder of just how important to our history and cultural heritage are the 'Punch and Judy People' of Merseyside.

NEW BRIGHTON'S GUINNESS FESTIVAL CLOCK

During the summer of 1951, the gloom and austerity of post-war Britain was dispelled temporarily with the staging of the Festival of Britain. To celebrate the 100th anniversary of the 1851 Great Exhibition, which had been held in Hyde Park, a similar display of British achievements in science, technology, art and culture was staged on London's South Bank and at Battersea Pleasure Gardens.

It was here, in the fairground, that the first Guinness Festival Clock was built, as the brewery's contribution to the fun atmosphere of the Festival. This proved to be so popular that versions of it were soon erected in seaside towns around Britain, including at New Brighton in the grounds of the Tower Buildings and fairground.

This 25ft high heavily ornamented and brightly painted clock tower with adjoining Toy Town-like wooden caravan stood on public display, still and silent. That is until every fifteen minutes, when it burst into frenzied, colourful, cartoonlike and exciting life with animated characters familiar from the Guinness posters and television adverts. This provided an unusual and entertaining show for the large crowd that had gathered around it in eager anticipation.

A Guinness Festival Clock in full flow.
(Discover Liverpool library)

With a recorded musical accompaniment throughout, the performance began when doors opened in the centre of the clock tower. This showed a revolving stage that revealed four set pieces in turn, each one showing Guinness in a different season of the year. Meanwhile, windows opened in the front of the adjoining caravan to show a uniformed and harassed zookeeper being chased by various animals. In his hand the keeper had a bottle of Guinness as he ran past the window followed by the animals in a long line, who then all disappeared from view.

A few moments later, the keeper and the animals all reappeared but now running in the other direction. This time a large brown bear was in front and holding the Guinness bottle, with the keeper bringing up the rear and doing the chasing. At that moment a large sun on a spur to the right of the clock tower began to spin around as other animated scenes began to operate. These included the animal keeper now rising from under an umbrella, an ostrich emerging from a chimney, marionettes revolving around a whirligig, the Mad Hatter coming out of his house, and, finally, two toucans emerging to peck at a tree with watches and Guinness bottles hanging from it – the 'Guinness Time Tree'.

The show lasted for five minutes, after which the doors, windows and other moving parts all began to close up. Then the clock and caravan stood still and silent once more. But only for another fifteen minutes, when the entire spectacle would begin again. The New Brighton Guinness Clock operated until 1966, when all the clocks were taken down. One does remain, albeit a miniature version, in the Guinness Museum in Dublin.

King Kong of Mossley Hill

On the site of what are now university halls of residence at the top of Mossley Hill in Liverpool stood, in 1932, the Third Liverpool Zoological Garden on Woodlands Road. This had been founded by local animal importer, William Cross, but it was managed quite incompetently by his cousin, Mr H.E. Rogers.

Among the birds on view at the zoo were an Andean condor, a Griffon vulture, some flamingos, divers and trumpeters, and a kookaburra. The animals included a giant tortoise, jungle cats, woolly monkeys, golden lion marmosets and 'Simla', a 30-year-old, 4-ton Burmese elephant. Simla had come to the zoo from a circus and he danced to music played on gramophone records.

But the most popular creature in the zoo was 'Mickey' the chimp. He was a cantankerous, moody male chimpanzee who weighed 13 stone. He was bigger than a man and all muscle, and had an adventurous personality. Mickey repeatedly escaped from the zoo, and on one such bid for freedom he jumped the 8ft-high zoo wall into the road. When a coal cart driver attempted to intercept him he simply threw the man across the road, followed by his coal shovel.

The ape then kissed a woman who had greeted him by name – Mickey was a well-known and popular feature of the district – and then accompanied her some way down the road with his arm around her. He next started to paint some railings in Lugard Road, where astonished painters had just stopped to have a cup of tea. Mickey then wrenched batons from the hands of policemen who had arrived and were attempting to apprehend him. He only 'came quietly' when offered an orange held out to him by another woman – Mickey the chimp clearly had a 'thing' for the ladies!

Mickey was a continual source of entertainment for the paying public, especially when he played football, which he seemingly enjoyed. He even had his own favourite football. His party piece was to stand in goal whilst would-be strikers tried to score. They seldom did, though, because Mickey was a highly skilled goalie. Sadly though, more than one frustrated 'Dixie Dean' aimed directly at Mickey, deliberately trying to hurt and provoke him with the tough, leather footballs. Mickey would then throw the ball back at those who hurt him, much to the amusement of the crowd, but to the frustration and humiliation of the poor ape.

One such nasty encounter with the public provoked Mickey into his fourth and final escape on 24 March 1938. This time, though, the ape's actions were not so benign. He leapt the zoo wall and made his way into the playground of nearby Sudley Primary School. Here, the children were doing their PE exercises under the supervision of their teacher, Mr Gall. The brave teacher placed himself between the ape and the children to protect them, and was quite badly gashed in the neck and thigh by Mickey, who then hurled the 24-year-old young man, unconscious, across the playground.

Within a few moments, though, the teacher came round, and saw that the chimp was still in the yard, but Mickey then bounded over the schoolyard wall into the nearby road, and so the teacher and the children made it safely inside the school building. Mickey then climbed on to the roof of 29 Lugard Road, where fifteen policemen, a lion tamer, a zookeeper, four police cars, a Black Maria and even a coal merchant all arrived to recapture him. Immediately the coal merchant tried to coax him down, whether or not this was the tradesman from the previous encounter I have been unable to establish, neither can I say how he intended to persuade the chimp to leave his roof. I presume he had some bananas to hand as I cannot imagine that half a ton of nutty slack would have done the trick!

Nevertheless, all attempts failed and Mickey now began to tear slates from the roof and hurl them into the street. As he was now clearly dangerous Mickey was shot and severely wounded in the throat by armed policemen. He rolled off the roof and fell into the yard at the rear of the property. In great pain, witnesses watched as he crawled into a corner of the yard whimpering, and reached out for an old discarded football just like the one he cherished at the zoo. He then slowly pulled the ball towards him. At this point Major C.J. Bailey of the 38th Anti-Aircraft Battalion arrived from nearby Fulwood Army Barracks. He fired two shots at the pitiful ape, which at last ended Mickey's suffering and tragic life.

Coincidentally, and remarkably, just five years before Mickey's final escape from the zoo a film had taken the cinemas by storm. *King Kong* was the tale of a great ape. The creature is captured by an exploitative impresario and then put on humiliating display to perform for an uncaring public. Driven to escape by his mistreatment the ape then rampages around the streets and ends up at the summit of a high building. Here, he is shot and killed. He falls to the ground as a pitiful remnant of what nature had intended him to be. Like Mickey, King Kong had a thing for the ladies. But at least Mickey did not take one of them up on the roof with him!

Mickey's escape, plus other incidents at the zoo, finally forced the authorities to close it down in 1938. But, not wanting to miss a financial opportunity, Cross and Rogers had Mickey stuffed and mounted, complete with his football. He was placed on display in the basement of Lewis's department store in Liverpool town centre, where people paid 6*d* a time to see the body of the famous chimpanzee.

When Lewis's store was destroyed by Nazi bombing during the May Blitz of 1941, so too was Mickey the chimp, and Liverpool's own 'King Kong' was gone forever.

Mickey the chimp ends his days being stuffed and mounted.
(Courtesy of Ken Rogers and the *Liverpool Echo*)

Select Bibliography

A Guide to Liverpool 1902, Liverpool Libraries & Information Service, 2004

A Nonagenarian, *Recollections of Old Liverpool*, Echo Library, 2009

Bailey, F.A. and Millington, R., *The Story of Liverpool*, Corporation or the City of Liverpool, 1957

Baines, Edward and Parson, William, *History, Directory and Gazetteer of the County Palatine of Lancashire*, Volume 2, Nabu Press, 2012

Buildings of Liverpool, Liverpool Heritage Bureau, 1978

Cavanagh, Terry, *Public Sculpture of Liverpool*, Liverpool University Press, 1997

Chandler, George, *Liverpool*, 1957

Chappell, Gavin, *Wirral Smugglers, Wreckers and Pirates*, Countyvise Ltd, 2009

Charters, David, *Great Liverpudlians*, Palatine Books, 2010

Chitty, Mike, *Discovering Historic Wavertree*, Wavertree Society, 1999

Colville, Quintin, and Davey, James (eds), *Nelson, Navy and Nation*, Conway, 2013

Cooper, John Gerard, *Liverpool Firsts*, Sigma Leisure, 1997

Doyle, Peter, *Mitres and Missions in Lancashire*, The Bluecoat Press, 2005

Hand, Charles, *Olde Liverpoole and its Charter*, Book Clearance Centre, 2005 reprint edition

Hatton, Peter B., *The History of Hale*, 1991

Hinchliffe, John, *Liverpool: Maritime Mercantile City*, University of Chicago Press, 2009

Hird, Frank, *Old Lancashire Tales*, Memories, 2000

—, *Old Merseyside Tales*, Book Clearance Centre, 2000

Hollinghurst, Hugh, *Classical Liverpool*, Liverpool History Society, 2008

—, *John Foster and Sons: Kings of Georgian Liverpool*, Liverpool History Society, 2009

Hollinshead, Janet E., *Liverpool in the Sixteenth Century*, Carnegie Publishing Ltd, 2007

Hudson, Roger (ed.), *Nelson and Emma*, The Folio Society, 1994

Hughes, Quentin, *Liverpool, City of Architecture*, The Bluecoat Press, 1999

Jackson, W.C.M., *Herdman's Liverpool*, The Gallery Press, 1968

Jones, Ron, *The Beatles' Liverpool*, Liverpool History Press, 2016

Lewis, David, *The Churches of Liverpool*, The Bluecoat Press, 2001

Liverpool, Birkenhead and New Brighton, Ward Lock & Co., 1917

Liverpool History Society Journals (various issues)

Melville, Herman, *Moby Dick*, William Collins, 2013

—, *Redburn: His First Voyage*, CreateSpace Independent Publishing Platform, 2013

Moore, Jim, *Underground Liverpool*, The Bluecoat Press, 1998

Nicholson, Susan N., *The Changing Face of Liverpool, 1207–1727*, National Museums & Galleries on Merseyside, 1982

Noel-Stevens, Jo, *The Hidden Places of Lancashire and Cheshire*, M & M Publishing Ltd, 1991

Pearce, Joseph P., *Romance of Ancient Leverpoole*, Philip, Son & Nephew Ltd, 1933

Power, Michael (ed.), *Liverpool Town Books 1649–1671*, 1999

Richardson, Andrew F., *Well I Never Noticed That!* Parts 1 and 2, West Derby Publishing

Rimmer, Ralph, *Around Wallasey and New Brighton*, Nonsuch Publishing, 2006

Stonehouse, James, *The Streets of Liverpool*, British Library, 2011

Whale, Derek, *Lost Villages of Liverpool*, Parts 1, 2 and 3, T.Stephenson & Sons Ltd, 1984

Williams, Peter Howell, *Liverpolitana*, Merseyside Civic Society, 1971

Wong, Maria Lin, *Chinese Liverpudlians*, Liver Press, 1989

Plus a range of resources provided by the Internet.

ABOUT THE AUTHOR

Born and bred in Liverpool, Ken Pye FRSA has recently retired as the Managing Director of The Knowledge Group. In a varied career spanning over forty-five years, Ken has experience in all professional sectors. This includes working as a Residential Child Care Officer for children with profound special needs; as a Youth and Community Leader; as the Community Development Officer for Toxteth; the North-West Regional Officer for Barnardo's; the National Partnership Director for the Business Environment Association; and Senior Programme Director with Common Purpose.

However, he continues as Managing Director of Discover Liverpool. As such, ken is a recognised expert on the past, present and future of

The author. (Liverpool Athenaeum library)

his home city and is a frequent contributor to journals, magazines and newspapers. He is also a popular after-dinner speaker and a guest lecturer to a wide range of groups and organisations. He is also a regular broadcaster for both radio and television. Ken is a Fellow at Liverpool Hope University and a Fellow of the Royal Society of Arts.

Well known across Merseyside and the North-West, Ken is the author of over ten books on the history of his home city and its city region, and is a widely recognised expert in his field. Ken's works include *Discover Liverpool* and *The Bloody History of Liverpool*; *A Brighter Hope*, about the founding and history of Liverpool Hope University; two volumes of his anthology of *Merseyside Tales*; *Liverpool: The Rise, Fall and Renaissance of a World Class City*; *An A to Z of Liverpool* and *Liverpool Pubs*.

Having also completed two private writing commissions for the Earl of Derby, Ken has just issued his set of four audio CDs, on which he tells his stories of the *Curious Characters and Tales of Merseyside*.

On a personal basis, and if pressed (better still, if taken out to dinner), Ken will regale you with tales about his experiences during the Toxteth Riots; as a bingo caller; as a puppeteer; as the lead singer of a 1960s pop group and as a mortuary attendant.

Ken is married to Jackie and they have three children: Ben, Samantha and Danny.

Visit Ken's website at www.discover-liverpool.com

Visit our website and discover thousands of other History Press books.

www.thehistorypress.co.uk